CRAFTING DIGITAL WRITING

Composing Texts Across Media and Genres

TROY HICKS

HEINEMANN
Portsmouth, NH

Heinemann
361 Hanover Street
Portsmouth, NH 03801–3912
www.heinemann.com

Offices and agents throughout the world

The author and publisher wish to thank those who have generously given permission to reprint borrowed material:

Figure 3.3: An example of a Hacked Website Image on the Heinemann website. Website page used by permission of Heinemann.

Figure 4.3: Screenshots of Prezi platform with student work "Macbeth." Used by permission from Prezi, Inc.

Figure 5.1: Screenshot of the Aviary Project File for the book trailer for *Artemis Fowl: The Lost Colony*. Used by permission of Aviary.

Table 5.4: How to Save an Audio Text to a Website and a Web-based Service. AudioBoo screenshots used by permission of Audioboo.

Figures 8.2, 8.3, and 8.4: Screenshots from "Earth and Its Layers" Video Game made with Gamestar Mechanic. Used by permission of Gamestar.

Figure 8.5: Cover of *The Westing Game* by Ellen Raskin. Used by permission of Penguin Group (USA) Inc. All rights reserved.

Cataloging-in-Publication Data is on file with the Library of Congress
ISBN: 978-0-325-04696-9

Editor: Tobey Antao
Production editor: Sonja S. Chapman
Typesetter: Eric Rosenbloom, Kirby Mountain Composition
Cover and interior designs: Monica Ann Crigler
Manufacturing: Steve Bernier

Printed in the United States of America on acid-free paper
17 16 15   EBM   3 4 5

S.
Thank you for being my biggest fan.
T.

CONTENTS

CHAPTER 5: Crafting Audio Texts   87

CHAPTER 6: Crafting Video Texts   104

CHAPTER 7: Crafting Social Media   137

CHAPTER 8: Modeling and Mentoring the Digital Writing Process   154

FOREWORD

I remember the day my father brought home an early model Apple Macintosh computer he was loaned from his job at Allen-Bradley. An enormous beige box, it looked like a stack of toasters three high and two deep. He plopped it on the wobbly maroon card table he and my mother put up in the family room to hold this magical new machine. My sister and I stood next to him transfixed as he booted it up. For as outdated as that giant humming box seems today, it was a gateway into hours and hours of learning that felt like play. Well before the Internet was even a thing, we toyed around with fonts and layouts, designed interactive stories, created dot-matrix posters galore. That Macintosh opened up a world not just of creation but of belief in our own ability. What you saw in your mind you could make for others to see. It was more than creativity, it was empowering.

Flash-forward to today; I remain deeply in love with technology yet feel a major rift between my out-of-school swiping and clicking and my in-school instruction. Partly because I just haven't done it enough: blogs and vlogs and something called Glogs at times feel like a foreign language and just as I start to get a handle on one I hear of fifty more that are supposedly better. Partly this rift exists for me because, to be honest, I worry about technology becoming a thing to do just to do it. A full class period swiping tiles around on a SMART Board has struck me at times as not much different than a period doing crosswords or watching a movie; sure it's fun but where is the learning?

I have struggled to unite my app-loving, content-making self with my literacy-empowering, student-centered self.

Luckily, there is Troy Hicks.

Troy stands for the kind of learning, engagement, and development I want for all children. He sees technology as not just something students play with the last period of the day before a vacation, but as an integral part of strong literacy teaching and learning. That creating a video documentary, for example, uses many of the same muscles as writing an informational essay and then some. That in our world today, design is intimately connected with content. That for students technology can be the invitation to dive deeply into writing craft.

What I love about *Crafting Digital Writing* is that it is a living, learning, interactive book. It is one you will want your laptop open for. Trust me on this one. I began reading on a plane and within moments was desperate to return to the ground so I could click each and every link to digital resources and thumb through the abundance of student samples. It is more than a book, it is a conversation—one Troy orchestrates between researchers, teachers, students, and you, all around the art of digital literacy for the sake of literacy.

I left reading, clicking, and furiously making notes, with a sense that I *could* explore the power of digital literacy instruction with students and, more important, asking myself why I haven't started sooner.

—Christopher Lehman

ACKNOWLEDGMENTS

Somewhere, somehow, and in some way, my work as a teacher and writer has been influenced by thousands of people. I know it is cliché, yet such is the joy and challenge of teaching; we never quite know where our influence begins or ends. Still, I can safely say that I have had many conversations with mentors, colleagues, students, and friends about digital writing over the past two years while writing this book, and each has helped shape my view. A little here, a lot there. It all adds up. From my immediate family and closest friends, to the students and colleagues I work with at Central Michigan University, and through the broader network of teachers and teacher educators that I meet through workshops, conferences, Twitter chats, webinars, email exchanges, and pure luck, I could easily fill pages and pages of acknowledgments for this book. I want to offer my broadest and most genuine thanks to those with whom I've worked over the past fifteen years in my career as an educator, knowing that our conversations will continue. I also want to offer just a few specific acknowledgments here.

The time that it takes to write a book is time borrowed from other people in our lives, most notably our spouses and children. For their patience during my hectic work and writing schedule, I love and appreciate my wife, Sara, and our blended family that includes Tyler, McKenna, Lexi, Beau, Shane, and Cooper. I talk about our "Brady Bunch" during my presentations, and you have been gracious enough to provide examples of your own writing for me to share with the world. Sorry that this one isn't a picture book, but I'm still working on that part of my writing repertoire!

For this particular book, Tobey Antao has mentored and supported me from the proposal process all the way through the final draft. Good editors ask smart questions and, if you're lucky, provide some support and encouragement along the way. Great editors ask you the questions that are much more difficult to answer, push you to explore new topics, and help you discover something about yourself as a writer. Exceptional editors become trusted friends and mentors. Tobey is exceptional, and the shape of this book is truly a result of her persistence and vision.

There are times in our lives when we feel absolutely compelled to say something, and times in our lives when we aren't sure that anything we have to say will be valuable. While twenty years ago I can't imagine that he would have been proud of me for writing anything short of a textbook on electrical engineering, I have to thank my dad, Ron Hicks, for his continued interest in my work as an English teacher. More important, he knows how to ask simple question such as "How's the book going?" in a genuine way, never imparting an undue expectation and instead asking with eager anticipation. The past few years have been difficult for our family, and yet he continues to help me find the strength to keep writing, even if there aren't any elaborate equations or crafty calculations. For that, I love and thank him.

INTRODUCTION

1

Being creative involves doing something. It would be odd to describe as creative someone who never did anything. To call somebody creative suggests that they are actively producing something in a deliberate way. (Robinson 2011, 142)

Every writing teacher enjoys finding a brilliant example of author's craft, a turn of phrase or line of dialogue that a student has created showing a spark of personality, a smart insight, or a unique way of presenting a character, setting, situation, or argument. These are the moments we strive for in our teaching, conferring, and evaluating. We share mentor texts to help students see how it can be done, and when it happens for our student writers, we celebrate those insightful uses of language. As Ken Robinson reminds us, creativity is about more than luck; it involves intention, deliberation, and selecting from among choices.

In short, crafting writing is an act of creativity.

Our rich history of teaching writing through a workshop approach (Atwell 1998, 2002; Calkins 1994; Calkins, Hartman, and White 2005; Fletcher 1992, 2010; Fletcher and Portalupi 1998, 2001; Fountas and Pinnell 2012; Graves and Kittle 2005; Kittle 2008; Lane 1992, 1999; Portalupi and Fletcher 2001; Ray 1999; Ray and Laminack 2001), as well as research supporting the effectiveness of teaching writing in this manner (Graham and Perin 2007; National Council of Teachers of English 2008; National Writing Project and Nagin 2006), provides us, as teachers in the second decade of the twenty-first century, with strong incentive to continue using a workshop approach that invites writers to explore author's craft, confer with us and their peers, and publish their work for a variety of audiences. In addition, studies of youth culture show the ways our children are adapting to digital media, and participating in a variety of virtual communities (Ito et al. 2009). In classrooms across the country, teachers continue to invite their students to explore the ways in which their words and ideas can come to life through letters and words. This is important work, no doubt. No one—not even a "digital" person like me—should ever argue that we entirely give up crayons, pencils, ink, and paper, especially with our youngest writers.

Yet it is clear that student writers in the twenty-first century are doing much more than alphabetic print on paper; they are increasingly exploring images, videos, slideshows, wikis, podcasts, digital stories, and other types of digital writing that allow them to share their work beyond their classroom walls with other students, their parents, and the broader audiences that the Internet allows (Beach, Anson, Breuch, and Swiss 2008; Herrington, Hodgson, and Moran 2009; Hicks 2009; Kajder 2010; Kist 2009; National Writing Project, DeVoss, Eidman-Aadahl, and Hicks 2010; Richardson 2010). More recently, the approach of studying different genres has gained traction in K-12 settings as well (Dean 2008; Fleischer and Andrew-Vaughan 2009; Lattimer 2003). As writing continues to shape and be shaped by digital tools and networked spaces, and as standards for teaching and learning how to write broaden to encompass new genres and media, writers are presented with more and more options. The question is no longer whether we *should* use technology to teach writing; instead we must focus on the many ways that we *must* use technology to teach writing.

For some teachers and students, technology provides the real audiences, purposes, and publication venues that allow them to grow their communities of writers, to discover digital writing, and to invite parents and families into the process. Whether they have one computer in their classroom and limited access to additional technology or are fortunate enough that every student has a laptop, many teachers are providing students with opportunities to be readers and writers of digital texts. While the hype about twenty-first-century literacies may sometimes be overwhelming, these digital skills and the habits of mind they foster have become, at the very least, a pointed topic in our current discussions of educational practice and policy and, at best, a way for students to truly understand what it means to be literate in their ever more digital world.

A quick example can inform our understanding of youth culture and literacy practices. Figure 1.1 contrasts the many types of writing Tyler Peterson, a student of Chris Sloan's, in Salt Lake City, Utah, finds in school with the one device he uses

Tyler Peterson's Photo Composition for Digital Learning Day 2012

Figure 1.1

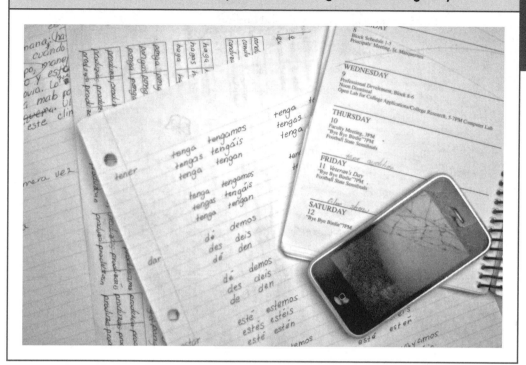

to connect to the world. He created this photo as a response to Digital Learning Day in the winter of 2012. His composition makes me wonder:

- What do you notice as you study the way Tyler crafted the composition of this photo? What are the ways in which he uses writing as a tool for learning?

- What types of literacy practices are most dominant in school? What technologies—both the tools as well as the formats—of writing are most evident? Why?

- On the other hand, what types of literacy practices are most dominant outside school? How does the use of a particular technology that allows for customization and interaction compare and contrast with the tools and formats available in school?

- As we continue to think about the ways that students engage with digital media, what are the advantages and disadvantages of both traditional, academic literacies and newer, digital ones?

Tyler's photo composition raises some questions and concerns relative to digital writing practices in school. Let me deal with a few of them. First, sadly, not all students have reasonable access to technology—many don't have any access at all—despite the proliferation of mobile devices across the United States and around the world. Second, yes, technologies can be fragile; Tyler somehow cracked the screen on his smartphone, and not all students would be able to afford even a reasonable insurance policy. Third, I agree, there is something reassuring about the tangible feel of paper in one's hand. Finally, we still face standardized tests.

Nevertheless, even though many of us are still teaching in an analog world—and the concerns noted above are real ones—research in the fields of digital writing and adolescent literacy shows that students become more engaged when we invite them to compose with digital media. Being intentional about that work by helping students understand the creative process of digital composition thus becomes our biggest challenge and most pertinent task as teachers of writing.

Overview of the Book

In *The Digital Writing Workshop* (2009), I articulated a vision for how to combine digital writing (writing that is produced using various electronic media and shared online) with the writing workshop approach described above. Over the past few years, as I have worked with teachers in my own writing project and various professional development venues around the country, many versions of the same question kept popping up: *I understand that we must ask our students to write with technology, and you are giving us some interesting examples, but how do we really* do *it?* Moreover, teachers seem to ask this in a way that implies the underlying question, *Is this really writing?*

Here, in *Crafting Digital Writing*, we will explore how to teach digital writing by examining author's craft in much more detail. I assume that you, as a teacher and reader, agree that teaching digital writing is our responsibility and our challenge. This book moves forward from there, focusing on *how* we should teach students to craft digital writing and, in the process, demonstrates that this really is writing and worthy of our attention in school. With the gracious help of many teacher colleagues and their students, I explain how intentional thinking about author's craft in these digital texts makes them engaging and effective. I see the use of digital writing as a both/and, not an either/or, proposition. Students still need to write academic texts, yes; but they can learn how to write those texts while also creating digital texts, and their learning should benefit from the reciprocal processes. The remainder of this book delves deeper into various aspects of author's craft through different forms of digital writing.

Chapter 2: Author's Craft, Genre Study, and Digital Writing

This chapter uses a recent publication by the Council of Writing Program Administrators, the National Council of Teachers of English, and the National Writing Project—*Framework for Success for Postsecondary Writing* (2011)—as a lens through which we can think about the elements of author's craft in texts that are "born digital," as well as the writing standards in the Common Core State Standards (Common Core State Standards Initiative 2010).

Chapter 3: Crafting Web Texts

Reading on the web has become a primary way for us to gather information. But what about writing for the web? How do we teach students to craft effective web-based texts with tools such as blogs, wikis, and websites? By examining two types of student projects—digital essays produced with Google Docs and a wiki as well as a wiki-based science journal—this chapter explores the elements of web-based texts that incorporate images, links, and other multimedia elements.

Chapter 4: Crafting Presentations

Slideshow presentations are now ubiquitous in classrooms as well as boardrooms, but we often fail to move beyond templates and bulleted lists. How can we help students design effective slideshows and, moreover, use other forms of digital writing to craft effective presentations that move beyond slides alone? This chapter considers alternative ways—from zooming slideshows to interactive posters and timelines—of presenting ideas with different forms of digital writing.

Chapter 5: Crafting Audio Texts

Sounds surround us every day, and many messages come to us only through audio. This brief chapter explores the craft of different kinds of audio texts and discusses how digital writers can combine narration, music, and sound effects to create unique listening experiences.

Chapter 6: Crafting Video Texts

Nearly everyone carries a digital camera (or at least a mobile phone with a camera). While quick snapshots and videos uploaded to our favorite social networks can be fun, this chapter explores how we can more intentionally craft digital writing by using still and moving images. It includes examples of student documentary films and argumentative essays.

Chapter 7: Crafting Social Media

People are increasingly communicating with social media, with many positive outcomes but also sometimes negative consequences. How can we help our students develop deliberate approaches to sharing their digital writing through social media and, more important, read, view, listen, and respond to the work of their peers?

Chapter 8: Modeling and Mentoring the Digital Writing Process

The final chapter examines a series of digital writing examples from a single student as a way for us to see how we can teach with intention and creativity. Following this chapter, the book's appendixes include some tools for designing digital writing assignments and a quick guide to websites and apps for digital writing.

Toward Intentional Writing Instruction

At the risk of being presumptuous, my sincere hope is that this book, at this time, can be part of what Malcolm Gladwell (2002) calls a "tipping point"—when the ubiquity of digital writing and the pressures on public education force us (educators, parents, policymakers, and community members) to make a substantive change in the form and function of schools. Sizable questions, concerns, and challenges exist for educators taking up digital literacies in addition to, and sometimes in place of, traditional literacies. I recognize these as legitimate concerns and want to offer responses.

For instance, a number of recent books describe how we are wallowing in "the shallows" (Carr 2010), raising the "dumbest generation" (Bauerlein 2008), and feeling increasingly "alone together" in our networked world (Turkle 2011). These authors all make cogent arguments, and we do need to be wary of how our students use digital media and of the possibility they will become entrapped in their own "filter bubbles" (Pariser 2011). My intention is not to suppress the arguments these critics may have, some of which warrant a good deal of further discussion. But we also need to understand our students and their literate lives; recent work by Jeff Grabill suggests that many college freshmen value the writing they do while texting and social networking more than any other kind (MSU News 2010). Instead, I want to understand these arguments against more technology, using them to offer a perspective that relies on good pedagogy to guide our decision making when teaching writing, especially digital writing.

As you begin this book, I ask you to consider two points about the teaching of writing that continue to guide me.

First, Calkins, in *The Art of Teaching Writing*, suggests

> *If one text can be used as an exemplar of many qualities of good writing, we can take the time to read it together for all the wondrous ways in which it affects us, and only then return to it in order to examine the ways in which it embodies particular qualities of writing. What is most important is that we and our students be moved by a book. (1994, 278)*

Imagine the word *digital* in front of *writing* and replace *book* with *composition*, then reread the quote. Mentors texts matter. We must find strong examples of digital writing that moves us, and then exploring the craft becomes essential. Using mentor texts has never been more important, as educators continue to remind us (Anderson 2011; Dorfman and Cappelli 2007, 2009; Gallagher 2011; Kittle 2008). This book provides a series of snapshots into what professionals and students are doing, right now, to craft digital writing. My hope is that these mentor texts will inspire you and your students to innovate with writing, too.

Second, Kelly Gallagher, in *Write Like This*, reminds us:

> *[O]f all the strategies I have learned over the years, there is one that stands far above the rest when it comes to improving my students' writing: the teacher should model by writing—and think out loud while writing—in front of the class. (2011, 15)*

Again, add *digital* in front of the first *writing* and *digitally* after the next two and reread. We know that writing in front of our students has never been easy. Add the complications of SMART Boards, projectors, tablets, Internet connections, and any number of other technologies that all need to be working properly for us to show our digital writing process, and it can be quite daunting to stand up in front of our students, trying to sound smart while composing something meaningful.

However, this should not stop us. Even if you don't consider yourself a digital expert in anything, you are a reader, a writer, and a teacher. That combination makes you more than qualified to talk about the craft of digital writing with your students. Exploring models and developing lessons about craft—as with all writing instruction—will provide writing instruction that resonates beyond one project or even one class.

Before We Begin

Having acknowledged some possible critiques and concerns, it is time to begin. Before going too much further, I want to say a few words about the use of digital features such as QR codes and hyperlinks, as well as some of the replacement images you will find throughout the text.

First, the links and QR codes. One of the interesting considerations in writing this book, at this moment in 2013, is whether and how I should produce this text not just for the printed page but also for the screen. I have had many people ask me whether this would be an e-book only; others have reminded me of the time they spent sitting at their keyboard checking out websites while reading *The Digital Writing Workshop*. While there were some e-readers in 2009 when I was finishing up that book, and early 2010 saw the introduction of the iPad, the computer market—

let alone digital reading and writing—continues to evolve, and my guess is that many more of you will be reading this book on-screen.

My first note to you as reader (as well as clicker, listener, and viewer) is that I have moved the resources from *The Digital Writing Workshop* from the Ning site I originally made for that book to a Wikispace available at http://digitalwritingworkshop .wikispaces.com/. This wiki also includes a page containing links to all the resources related to *Crafting Digital Writing*: http://digitalwritingworkshop.wikispaces.com/ Crafting_Digital_Writing.

Scan to view resources for *Crafting Digital Writing.*

Those links are great if you are reading on-screen and can click on them, but if you want to get to that site while reading a print version of the book, you have to do plenty of typing. Thus, for longer URLs, I will include a shortened URL and/or QR code that you can scan with your smartphone or tablet. For instance, you can visit the page of resources for this book with this shortened link (http://goo.gl/ FQc2z) or use your mobile device to scan the QR code provided here. Because I could fill up many pages with QR codes, I have created them only for URLs that are unwieldy, not for top-level domain names (such as www.google.com) that are easier to type in or search for quickly.

No matter your means of navigation, I encourage you to become a member of the Digital Writing Workshop Wiki and contribute your great examples of digital writing to the gallery I am curating there. One of the great pleasures I have found in writing for, teaching, and speaking to educators is that so many of you are willing to share examples of your own lessons and student work.

Student work—more accurately, students' fair use of existing copyrighted work—is the reason for the second note. Throughout the book, you will find entire images or sections of screenshots replaced with notations about the image that you will in full online. While the students' original use of these images can be seen online and would be considered a fair use of copyrighted material, we are not able to reproduce them in a book that, ultimately, is for commercial purposes. Questions about fair use and copyright are important and, to a large extent, context specific.

No matter how old your students are, or what kinds of projects they are working on, it is likely that they will run into questions about copyright. It is beyond the scope of this book to answer these complicated questions. To that end, I want to suggest a number of resources for discussing copyright, fair use, and Creative Commons with your students.

- Media education scholar Renee Hobbs has a variety of resources, most notably the book *Copyright Clarity: How Fair Use Supports Digital Learning* (2010) and its accompanying wiki (http://copyrightconfusion.wikispaces.com/) that offer a good deal of guidance on educational uses of copyrighted materials.

- Librarian Joyce Valenza has created a number of great resources for educators and students, especially her *Copyright Friendly* wiki (http://copyrightfriendly.wikispaces.com/). With numerous links to sources for images, video, audio, and music, this wiki is a great place for students to start a search for additional media to use in their digital writing projects.

- The Creative Commons search page continues to improve, with options for easily identifying CC-licensed sources of images, video, and music (http://search.creativecommons.org/). Also, the Internet Archive has a continually growing collection of materials including video, images, audio, and texts (http://archive.org/).

Use these resources to pursue your own path to learning about copyright and how best to teach these issues in your classroom.

I thank you for picking up (or downloading) *Crafting Digital Writing: Composing Texts Across Media and Genres*. The possibilities of composing with digital media are, quite literally, infinite, so let us begin exploring them now.

AUTHOR'S CRAFT, GENRE STUDY, AND DIGITAL WRITING

2

Traditionally, teachers *have modeled perfection and students have struggled to meet [these] standards. Today, as teachers move toward individualized instruction and collaborative learning, students struggle to create and meet their own standards of excellence; teachers are learning to model the struggle. (Lane 1992, 6)*

As I shared in *The Digital Writing Workshop*, one of my favorite quotes about author's craft comes from Ralph Fletcher and JoAnn Portalupi's popular book, *Craft Lessons*: "craft is the cauldron in which the writing gets forged" (1998, 3).

The image of a blacksmith pounding away on an anvil, sparks flying, the hammer sounding blows, seems at first a stark contrast to the writer working quietly, pen on paper (or fingers on keyboard). Yet I appreciate the image of the forge and a cauldron, where ideas mix, are heated, and then blend into something new, something strong. This is the process of writing, and craft surrounds it all, infused in each and every step. This is true for any words that appear on paper or screen and is also true of the images, sounds, and other forms of media we choose when composing digital texts.

Many, many teachers and writers offer insights into craft, and it is worth looking at some examples. Even those who don't name these ideas as "craft" explicitly help us develop a sense of what writing teachers mean when they describe this elusive idea. We often talk with students (and one another, for that matter) in loose terms about "adding details and examples" or "bringing out your voice." It can be challenging for students to figure out what we mean when we want them to add details and examples or voice. If we are going to ask for these elements as part of our students' writing, we at least owe them an explanation of what we are looking for and models of how the elements work.

In short, craft does not need to be clouded in vague language about mystical writing abilities, even though that might keep with the medieval theme of forges and cauldrons. As Barry Lane reminds us, we need to share our own struggles with students. Clearly, we can teach craft in writing. And we can teach craft in digital writing, too, even though the struggles are perhaps more confounding (yet so full of possibilities). While there are many to choose from, I want to look at the idea of craft through three metaphors, leading us to a better understanding of how to identify craft in digital texts.

Studying Craft with Lenses

One view of craft is to see it as a tool for looking. Fletcher and Portalupi (1998) elaborate on the idea of "reading like a writer," introducing the idea of lenses.

> *A student who starts reading like a writer can, with our guidance, begin tuning in to the craft—the how—of the text being read. When we help students get a feel for the setting, voice, tension, inner story, or recurring detail, we are helping them develop new lenses with which to revisit their own writing. Such lenses are critical if they are going to grow into the writers they want to be. (13)*

Lenses are an apt metaphor for thinking about craft, especially in an age of digital media, screens, and (soon) web-enabled glasses or goggles. Even the most skilled readers among our students may not have all the lenses they need to see the ways in which an author constructs a text. Even with the correct lenses, students don't always look through them without prompting. Once students do recognize some of these craft elements, they often require the skillful, intentional nudges of a teacher to turn these ideas from something a reader has read into something a writer can write.

Studying Craft by Slowing Down

Once a lens is in place, most often through prompts offered by you as a teacher, it is time to really examine the craft element. Katie Wood Ray, in *Wondrous Words* (1999), offers one technique for doing so.

> *We have to work backwards from what we see in a finished text to what we imagine the writer did to make it come out that way. Seeing and understanding craft in texts is [difficult] . . . so we will slow this part way down and really explore the meaning of craft in text. (28)*

Slowing down to notice craft hardly seems possible as the number of standards, grade-level texts, genres, and (quite often) students in our classrooms continues to increase. Yet taking time to notice is essential. What resonates in Ray's words is the idea of meaning—what meaning does this particular element of craft bring to you as a reader? Why does it matter, for instance, that a word is repeated or that a character is described in a certain manner? When writers begin to think intentionally about creating meaning in their readers' minds, they are beginning to master the craft of writing.

Studying Craft by Starting Small

Once we have looked through the lens and slowed down to identify and explore the related elements of craft, Elizabeth Hale suggests a third important way to teach craft: start small. Starting small applies both to the craft element and to the way you approach your students. Hale, in *Crafting Writers, K–6* (2008), says:

> *Specific craft techniques are what I consider to be the small building blocks of different aspects of good writing, such as description, voice, and sentence fluency. Teaching specific craft, whether it's through whole-class*

lessons or [individual] conferences, shows students one particular way to write at a time so that each one is small enough to hold in their hands and own. (11)

Ownership. Such a simple idea with such profound consequences. We must coach our students to rely on mentors, usually through whole-class instruction. However, we must also encourage them to move beyond models; we want them to take risks with their writing—as the best writers do—and yet have the supports in place to help them understand when they've made a mistake. We need to teach craft in a variety of ways, and most likely a number of times, to the whole class, to small groups, and to individuals. Only then will students truly understand and own the technique. As Hale and so many others remind us, we need to focus on one element at a time.

Studying Craft in Digital Writing

Put on the lenses. Slow down. Start small.

All good advice. So many more writers and teachers have discussed craft in metaphorical or strategy-based ways, and it is impossible to cite and summarize them all here. These three are succinct and useful ways for us to remember what to do when looking at craft.

Another popular approach to understanding broader elements of craft is through genre study. A number of teachers and researchers have focused on ways in which genre study can enhance writing instruction; two effective approaches are the Teacher's College Reading and Writing Project's *Units of Study* curriculum (Lucy Calkins et al.) for the elementary grades and Deborah Dean's *Genre Theory* for high school students. In addition, Fountas and Pinnell (2012) define their approach as follows:

> *By genre study, we mean more than just learning the specific characteristics of each genre. We mean helping students learn how to learn about genre from other writers—how to study the way writers use craft and conventions in communicating meaning to their readers. Students think*

about the writer's purpose and audience and notice the features that help
the writer achieve an effective communication. What is learned about
genre in this way is generative—it can be applied to all the reading and
writing students do for the rest of their lives. (7)

Genre study complements the study of author's craft in the sense that craft is one piece in a larger genre puzzle. As I explain more below, with the Common Core's new focus on the three main text types—narrative, informational, and argument—elements of genre study will continue to inform our teaching of author's craft. It is appropriate, and even necessary, to use some elements of craft in some genres, but not all elements work in all genres. For instance, an allusion may work in a narrative, but in an informational text the writer may want to be more specific and avoid an ambiguous word or phrase. To that end, Duke et al. (2011) warn that we can be too general in our instruction; thus, one of the five guiding principles in their genre-based approach to teaching reading and writing is to "[e]xplicitly teach genre-specific or genre-sensitive strategies" (18).

As a way to think about crafting texts, genre study gives us a broader perspective on what can be accomplished within a particular mode of writing, as well as helps us think about the affordances of particular media. As we look at examples of how teachers are using digital writing tools throughout this book, it is important to note the various, flexible ways in which these tools can be employed, both as individual elements of author's craft and as wider elements of a particular genre.

In the past decade, more and more teachers and researchers have also begun to argue that visual literacy is as important as traditional alphabetic literacy. Most notable are Steve Moline and Katie Wood Ray. Moline, in his second edition of *I See What You Mean: Visual Literacy K–8* (2011), builds on the first edition—in which he largely relied on hand-drawn examples of student work—to now demonstrate the many ways in which digital tools can help students develop charts, graphs, diagrams, maps, tables, and other genres of visual texts. Ray, in her recent book *In Pictures and In Words: Teaching the Qualities of Good Writing Through Illustration Study* (2010), turns her ever thoughtful eyes as a teacher of writing on the ways in which illustrators and authors work hand in hand to make meaning. She explains:

In classrooms where children compose meaningfully inside picture books,
teachers have created an amazing context in which to teach composition—

and at a much deeper level than perhaps anyone ever imagined possible with children so young. But to get at the really deep work, teachers must look at children's illustrating not as an afterthought or simply the means to another, more important end. To get the really deep composition work, teachers must understand illustrating in this way—as composition. And teachers must believe that if they teach into this work, they are helping children become the kinds of effective communicators the twenty-first century demands, "possessing a wide range of abilities and competencies, many literacies." (17)

Expanding our vision for why and how children illustrate their work—as a critical component of composition, not as a way to simply brainstorm or polish one's work—is a critical distinction. In an age where students can do an online image search for just about anything, it is even more important that we ask them (at least some of the time) to think carefully about how to create their own illustrations (especially for narrative texts) and other visuals (for informational and argumentative texts). How these visual compositions add meaning to the overall piece of writing is a question of craft.

Table 2.1 lists a number of terms associated with the craft of writing, garnered from the authors mentioned above and my own pedagogical toolbox acquired during many years of teaching writing. While it would be wonderful to cite each individual term by author, many of the terms have entered the general lexicon about teaching writing. I will, however, offer a generous nod to Ralph Fletcher for terms like "recurring line" and "hot spot," as well as to Barry Lane for terms for ones like "snapshots," "thoughtshots," "binoculars," and "digging potatoes." Definitions of craft are also informed by curricular guidelines, most notably the Common Core State Standards, and some of the language in the table is taken from those documents as well. My intent is that this collected list of craft elements will be a useful guide throughout the rest of this book, as well as a guide you can use in your own classroom.

Craft is key to good writing, whether that writing is words on a page or involves additional media. Moreover, the combinations through which we can teach author's craft are nearly endless. Such is the joy of language in its multiple forms as well as the joy of being a teacher of writing. Additional challenges present themselves when we shift our thinking about craft from paper to screen. I'll now extend these ideas to digital writing and think about the ways we can choose from among these elements to craft the most effective types of multimodal texts.

Table 2.1	Elements of Author's Craft and Genre Study

Narrative Texts	Informational Texts	Argumentative Texts
Story Elements ■ Point of view ■ Character ■ Narrator (reliable or unreliable) ■ Setting/scene ■ Dialogue Plot Sequence ■ Flashback/forward ■ Exposition ■ Conflict ■ Rising action ■ Climax ■ Falling action ■ Denouement Literary Devices ■ Imagery ■ Symbolism ■ Personification ■ Simile/metaphor ■ Onomatopoeia	General Format ■ Introduction ■ Subheadings/sections ■ Conclusion Organizational Patterns ■ Chronological ■ Problem/solution ■ Compare/contrast ■ Cause/effect ■ Pro/con Details and Examples ■ Relevant facts ■ Extended definitions ■ Quotations or examples ■ Domain-specific vocabulary ■ Illustrations or graphics	Introduction Claim Evidence ■ General knowledge ■ Historical facts ■ Quotations ■ Statistical data ■ Quotes from experts ■ Surveys ■ Primary source documents ■ Photos ■ Video clips ■ Journalistic media ■ Wikipedia Warrant ■ Reasoning for the evidence Rebuttal and Counterargument ■ Acknowledging limitations Conclusion
Writing Strategies	Other Craft Strategies	Crafting Visuals

General Features
■ Titles
■ Sentence and paragraph
  formats
■ Employing transitions
Parts of Speech
■ Active verbs
■ Specific nouns
■ Conjunctions
Grammar and Usage
■ Using punctuation for effect
■ Active vs. passive
	■ Repetition or
	  "recurring line"
	■ Creating a "hot spot"
	■ Getting playful with puns,
	  idioms, allusions
	■ Playing with time
	■ Binoculars
	■ Thoughtshots
	■ Snapshots
	■ Digging potatoes
		Types
		■ Diagrams
		■ Maps
		■ Graphs
		■ Illustrations
		Features
		■ Perspective
		■ Background
		■ Movement
		■ Details
		■ Light/dark
		■ Size and shape
		■ Exaggerated features
		■ Color and tone

More Than Words: Studying Author's Craft in Digital Writing

This book began with a quote from Ken Robinson about creativity and deliberation. His words are important because digital writing—like all writing over the course of human history—can be created with many degrees of intention. For instance, at this moment, I am writing this chapter in my home office. I try to limit the distractions around me, although emails continue to fill my inbox and student assignments are yet to be graded. (Somehow though they don't seem quite so overwhelming, because they are all Google documents, not an ominous stack on my desk.)

Different writing tasks abound, and my level of intention for (and attention to) each task is limited. When I write a grocery list, it is usually done in the chaos of our kitchen. An email can be composed almost anywhere, especially since I carry a smart phone in my pocket. For many people, status updates on Facebook or Twitter also come from their phones, often while on the go. How intentional—and ultimately how creative—any of us might be in the choices we make as writers depends on many factors. Sure, I could be witty with my to-do list, but I would be the only person to appreciate it. A status update, digital story, or for that matter a sentence in this book requires a certain degree of *savior faire* (and in the latter case, an understanding of my intended reader, who I hope has about the same knowledge of fancy foreign phrases as I do).

In examining the craft of digital writing, my intent is to open up our thinking about both what counts as "writing" in our classrooms and what counts as "quality" in the writing our students compose. We can't get caught up solely in the media students choose; it is easy to quickly slip down this slope and say that what I am proposing here is not so much the work of a writing teacher but is rather best left to the teacher of media arts and communications, or left to students to figure out on their own, outside of our language arts class. Instead, I argue that the types of craft elements we insist our students create in their alphabetic texts can be complemented—or, better yet, extended—by the types of craft elements we can use given the availability of digital writing tools. With digital writing, we need to think with words, of course; yet we also need to begin thinking like artists, web designers, recording engineers, photographers, and filmmakers. In other words, intentional choices about craft can lead to creative work in a variety of writing media.

Why do I think this about the craft of writing? Moreover, why do I ask you, as a writing teacher, to do the same? Quite simply, I want to see our "digital generation" live up to their potential as conscientious citizens and creative producers of text in all forms. Sure, they can post status updates quicker than most of us adults can pull out our phones. Yet inviting them to be intentional about the craft of digital writing is perhaps the best way to help them realize their potential in academic, social, political, and community contexts. When we talk and teach thoughtfully about the elements of digital writing—words, images, sounds, videos, links, and other media elements—we are helping them be purposeful and, in turn, helping them be creative. To put a finer point on this distinction: it is one thing to fire off a status update, upload a quick snapshot, or post a hastily recorded video. It is quite another to craft a blog post linked from your update, compose a thoughtful photograph using the rule of thirds, or combine and edit multiple video clips to achieve a certain effect in a very brief film. It's all about intention and helping students identify, explore, and employ author's craft.

As writing teachers, we have been helping students look at craft for quite some time. Anyone who has used a teaching resource created by the authors I've mentioned earlier has been thinking about craft. But perhaps we have been too focused on the mentors *we* value, and students are missing the mentors that surround *them*. Ralph Fletcher, in *Mentor Authors, Mentor Texts* (2011), suggests that we loosen the reins on how we present mentor texts to our students.

> *Instead of directing students to pay attention to this strategy or that technique, what if we invite them to look at these texts and enter into them on their own terms. This would give students more control, more ownership, and it would respect the transactional dynamic that is present whatever anybody reads anything. (5)*

This goes for digital texts, too. Since our students are surrounded by these texts, we can and should invite them to bring in their own exemplars. This is where their experience as consumers of multimedia can come in handy; there is no scarcity of digital texts in our world.

Moreover, if digital writing involves intention, then it also involves attention. In his recent book, *Net Smart: How to Thrive Online* (2012), Howard Rheingold describes five literacies for actively participating in social media, one being attention. Among many tips, he offers this:

> *Social media attention training requires understanding your goals and priorities (intentions), and involves asking yourself, at regular intervals, whether your current activity at any moment moves you closer to your goal or serves your higher priorities (attention). (247)*

In relation to digital writing, the idea is that we must be deliberate in what we type when we post to social networks, how we frame a photograph, how we edit video, or any other number of choices that affect the composition of our texts. Renee Hobbs (2011) elaborates on this idea by offering a five-part process that engages students in digital and media literacy: access, analyze, create, reflect, and act. In particular, I'm interested in the way she describes both the *analyze* and *create* components, using terms such as *message purpose*, *target audience*, *credibility*, *point of view*, *creativity*, and *composition techniques* (12). Moreover, as Sara Kajder often says in her presentations, students may be "tech comfy," but they are not necessarily "tech savvy." Being a digital native isn't enough, and Kajder (2003, 2010) also elaborates on the many academic skills that students should be cultivating through their use of digital literacies such as inquiry, evaluation, and synthesis across genres and media. Being intentional moves them closer to becoming active, informed citizens who craft messages in smart, productive ways.

Both as a teacher and as a parent, I listen carefully to the criticisms levied on this generation and want to make sure I am doing my part to encourage students, as writers, to make sense of the world in serious, yet creative ways. By teaching writing through a workshop approach, and by integrating the sensibilities of what it means to be "digital" in terms of both technology and citizenship, I truly believe that we have an opportunity to help this generation define themselves on their own terms. Rather than succumbing to narcissism and self-promotion, we can help them understand how, when, and why digital writing matters, both for them as individuals and for their families and communities.

To think more about how we can do this, I would like to reiterate an idea I elaborated on in great detail in *The Digital Writing Workshop*, MAPS:

- *Mode*: the genre of a text

- *Media*: the form(s) in which a text is created

- *Audience*: the reader, listener, or viewer of the text, both intended and incidental

- *Purpose*: the action the author takes, in both an academic and a personal sense

- *Situation*: the context for the writer herself or himself, as well as the demands of the writing task

MAPS helps us see the broader context of a writing assignment and also helps the writer determine when, how, and why he or she may choose to use a particular element of author's craft. For instance, it may be appropriate to include a joke that involves play on words in a personal narrative, but using the same play on words in an argument essay may not be as effective. Document design also matters when thinking about MAPS, especially the "media" component. As Bush and Zuidema (2011) argue

> *The decisions an author makes about how a page [or website, presentation, and other forms of text] looks can be as important as the text the document contains. Great text + weak design and weak text + great design will both have the same effect: a document that doesn't achieve its goals. (87)*

Using the MAPS heuristic is a way for us to think broadly about the contexts in which we write and, more important, to help our student writers reach their goals. Appendix A, "Creating a Digital Writing Assignment," offers some ideas for how I would use the MAPS heuristic and other resources as a guide for developing assignments that specifically focus on craft.

Throughout the remainder of this book, I talk about the traditional elements of author's craft listed in Table 2.1 in conjunction with the elements that comprise digital writing (see Table 2.2), all the while considering how MAPS affects the intended meaning. These additional elements help us focus the conversation on what a writer can do to make a message effective. For instance, we can talk about transitions in two ways: first, in using certain words and phrases to move between ideas in

Table 2.2	Additional Elements of Author's Craft in Digital Writing

Website Design	Audio
Typography ■ Serif and sans serif fonts ■ Font size and orientation ■ Kerning (distance between letters) Layout/Organization ■ Parent and child pages ■ Links (internal and external) Colors ■ Primary and complementary ■ Hot vs. cool Overall User Experience	Actual Sounds ■ Character's voices ■ Noises from within the story ■ Music from within the story, either played on an instrument or from a radio/device Commentary/Additional Sounds ■ Narrator or "voice of God" ■ Sounds added for effect ■ Music added for effect
Presentations	**Video**
Slide Design and Layout ■ Lines ■ Shape ■ Color ■ Texture ■ Space ■ Transitions and animations Information Graphics ■ Data ■ Symbols ■ Key ■ Data visualization Additional Images ■ Size ■ Orientation ■ Watermarks	Cinematic Techniques ■ Camera angle ■ Cuts/transitions ■ Focus (near, mid, far) ■ Framing ■ Gaze ■ Establishing shot ■ Pan ■ Zoom Documentary Techniques ■ Voice-over ■ Interviews ■ Archival footage ■ Reconstructions ■ Montage ■ Exposition

traditional texts and, second, while showing how links within a web-based text allow readers to move to different segments of a website (or, to use a different example, how certain camera angles and cuts from one scene in a film to the next can signal subtle—or stark—transitions). The combinations are infinite, which is one reason teaching digital writing compels me in the way it does. As writers ourselves, and as teachers of writing, what we know about crafting words on the page can be complemented by what we find in the techniques mentioned in Table 2.1, most of which come either from references mentioned later in the book as well as from Wikipedia entries about these topics.

In considering all these elements of author's craft—those taken from traditional writing as well as those that can be employed only in digital writing—we offer our students a broad range of choices. It is worth saying one more time that intention is the beginning of any well-crafted, creative piece of writing. Throughout the rest of this book, we will explore the choices that professional and student authors have made, thus thinking critically and creatively about ways to craft digital writing across genres and media.

Common Core Standards, Successful Writers, and the Struggle Ahead

One other element is woven throughout this book: the Common Core State Standards (CCSS). Given the focus in the CCSS on the three major text types (narrative, informational, and argument), the book's subtitle—*Composing Texts Across Media and Genres*—makes clear that teaching digital writing contributes to, and I hope extends, our understanding of what it means to teach writing. A few recent publications highlight some of the new challenges that we will face. First, Calkins, Ehrenworth, and Lehman (2012) remind us that the three major text types still allow us to explore numerous genres (103) and that even though no instructional plans are explicitly written into the CCSS,

> *[T]he Common Core writing standards seem utterly aligned to the writing process tradition that is well established across the states, with a few*

new areas of focus and a raised bar for the quality of writing we should expect students to produce. This quality of writing can be achieved by mandating the explicit instruction, opportunities for practice, centrality of feedback, assessment-based instruction, and spiral curriculum that have all been hallmarks of rigorous writing workshop instruction. (112)

In other words, high-quality writing instruction is still high-quality writing instruction, regardless of new curricular expectations. Given their focus on the writing process/writing workshop approach, I continue to align my thinking with Calkins and the other teachers of writing described in this book. My contribution, then, will be to discuss how we can do this work in a digital writing workshop approach.

These ideas are echoed more broadly in a number of other resources that suggest teaching writing is about more than simply putting words on the page. For instance, Zemelman, Daniels, and Hyde (2012) argue that "the Standards provide only a partial picture of good writing instruction. They focus on products we can see and measure, what the designers hope students can ultimately *do*" (137, emphasis in text). They go on to describe how the standards seem to encourage a skill-and-drill approach and that we, instead, need to utilize the writing process and teach from the approach of writing workshop.

In a similar manner, Beach, Thein, and Webb (2012) encourage us to "exceed" the CCSS and describe how literacy is more than the ability to encode and decode text. They suggest that "[s]tudents can adopt a variety of different perspectives to analyze how spaces and systems shaping events are constructed through historical, institutional/civic, cultural, psychological, and economic forces" (61). This critical approach to teaching language relies on a rich history of socio-cultural research and invites students to compose a variety of text types across a variety of media.

Finally, there are resources that focus on each major text type. A trio of authors—Wilhelm, Smith, and Fredricksen—have written three books, each of which takes a comprehensive view of one of the text types: narrative (Fredricksen, Wilhelm, and Smith 2012), argument (Smith, Wilhelm, and Fredricksen 2012), and informational (Wilhelm, Smith, and Fredricksen 2012). Each volume invites students to explore a variety of subgenres and writing approaches. Hillocks, too, has developed resources for crafting narrative (2006) and, more recently, argumentative writing (2011). Dorfman and Cappelli (2009) share lessons that lead to informational writing through the study of nonfiction mentor texts. (And, I am sure, there are undoubtedly many more sources of examples for narrative, informational, and argumentative writing that I have missed.)

I have so many colleagues—K–12 teachers, professional development staff, and university faculty—whom I could also hold up as exemplary writing teachers and mentors. In my regular interactions with preservice and practicing teachers, as well as language arts consultants and teacher educators, I am reminded that the CCSS can be seen as a burden; yet it also provides a unique opportunity for teachers throughout this nation to focus on the importance of teaching writing. Technology continues to play its role in this process, and there is not a writer in our classrooms today who will not be producing *something* with a digital writing tool in her or his lifetime. More important, to echo the call I made in *The Digital Writing Workshop*, I still believe in the mantra these writing teachers, especially Calkins, repeat, with my added corollary: teach the writer, then the writing, *then the technology*.

We find ourselves under very real constraints at this moment in education's history. What good will it do to teach with digital technologies when we teeter on the cusp of a new testing regimen that will increasingly focus our attention on producing argumentative essays that generally adhere to some variation of a five-paragraph format, with six-trait assessment? How will we keep digital writing—as well as analytical thinking, problem solving, and authentic assessment—in our writing classrooms? While I am not in a K–12 classroom every day, I work with teachers all the time and often hear about the constraints they face with regard to access, time, equipment, and testing. Your situation may be similar. Yet I also know that those of us who teach writing can no longer cling to the idea that producing good test-takers will yield the types of writers who will succeed in college, career, and life. Students today may be "born digital," but it is our job to help them become purposeful and creative digital writers.

As I've said, I would never want a child to lose his or her sense of what it means to focus on a small moment, write it down with pencil on paper, describe that moment in detail, and enjoy the praise received when he or she holds tightly to that paper, reading that story aloud to a trusted friend, teacher, or parent. I also know that this is only one of many forms of writing he or she will be asked to perform over a lifetime, both in school and out. I want students to be prepared for college and the workforce, and I also want them to have a good sense of themselves, both as writers and as individuals who will choose to represent themselves in a variety of ways, in a variety of contexts. Before moving into the chapters of this book that deal with the craft of digital writing, we can think about how best to accomplish these goals by looking at another framework for measuring a writer's success.

Among the numerous research reports, white papers, and curriculum documents that have surfaced in the past few years, I want to highlight a joint project released by the Council of Writing Program Administrators (CWPA), the National Council of Teachers of English (NCTE), and the National Writing Project (NWP). In a document titled *Framework for Success in Postsecondary Writing* (2011; http://wpacouncil.org/framework/), these three professional organizations summarize eight key attributes, or "habits of mind," our students need in order to attain "college and career readiness."

- *Curiosity*—the desire to know more about the world

- *Openness*—the willingness to consider new ways of being and thinking in the world

- *Engagement*—a sense of investment and involvement in learning

- *Creativity*—the ability to use novel approaches for generating, investigating, and representing ideas

- *Persistence*—the ability to sustain interest in and attention to short- and long-term projects

- *Responsibility*—the ability to take ownership of one's actions and understand the consequences of those actions for oneself and others

- *Flexibility*—the ability to adapt to situations, expectations, or demands

- *Metacognition*—the ability to reflect on one's own thinking as well as on the individual and cultural processes used to structure knowledge

The framework goes on to describe five different experiences that students could have with writing, reading, and critical analysis, two of which are particularly notable given the topic of this book: "developing flexible writing processes" and "composing in multiple environments." For me, as well as many other teachers with whom I have explored this document, the most notable feature of these habits of mind is that they do not break down into "measurable" standards applicable to a particular rubric or checklist. Instead, they offer a way to talk about the work writers do. These conversations can happen between us, as colleagues, and, more important, between our students and us as teachers. If we use these habits of mind as conversation starters when talking about the craft of writing, as well as when analyzing mentor texts and reflecting on our own writing processes, they become another important set of lenses through which we can view and discuss writing.

The struggle that all writers have faced—whether with quill and parchment, chalk and slate, or pen and paper—are the struggles our students still face with digital texts. They are yearning to tell their stories, show us how, or make a point, regardless of the media they use to craft the writing. We can help them embrace these habits of mind while meeting the standards. That is the goal of teaching craft, and throughout this book, I will build on this idea by specifically focusing on the intentional and creative work that students do when they create a variety of texts, texts that are born digital. Using elements of traditional author's craft (Table 2.1), the elements of author's craft in digital texts (Table 2.2), and the *Framework*'s "habits of mind," Chapters 3–7 examine what it means to create a variety of text types in different media, beginning with web-based texts.

CRAFTING WEB TEXTS

We believe that to be literate in the twenty-first century, students must become composers and readers of hypermedia. They must understand its possibilities, uses, and design. Since our future texts, even more so than our current ones, will be hypertextual, students will need to understand the conventions and construction of such texts. (Wilhelm, Friedemann, and Erickson 1998, 20)

As few as ten or fifteen years ago, producing a web page—whether just alphabetic text or something more sophisticated with images, audio, or video—to post on the Internet was a fairly complicated procedure. While being able to type text on the computer keyboard made some aspects of publishing a bit faster, for the average user it was usually a multistep process to get a photo scanned, converted, and sized just right. Don't get me started on converting video!

The person hoping to post a web page containing a combination of text, images, and video had to have the appropriate kinds of software on her computer (some of which was free, but most of which cost a good deal of money) and access to a web domain (sometimes available through school or work but often needing to be purchased at a hefty price). It is hard to imagine having to sit in front of a dedicated computer, with FTP (file transfer protocol) access to a server and plenty of time to learn HTML (hypertext markup language). To produce a professional-looking website, a digital writer would likely not have relied on available tools and spaces such as the rudimentary (and often tacky) Angelfire or Tripod, but instead would have used sophisticated software like Dreamweaver or FrontPage. Maintaining consistency across the individual pages of an entire website took either lots of individual updates or understanding how to create templates. Publishing web-based texts took time, effort, and expertise.

Since blogs, wikis, and video- and audio-sharing sites emerged in the early 2000s and "push-button publishing" became the dominant form of publication on the web, becoming an author and sharing one's work with the world is within reach of anyone who can connect to the Internet. The WYSIWYG (what you see is what you get) text editor is a popular web-based tool, and today's digital writers will quite likely never experience hand-coding HTML or uploading files via FTP.

Instead, we are able to use tools such as Blogger (www.blogger.com), Word-Press (http://wordpress.com), Tumblr (www.tumblr.com), Wikispaces (www .wikispaces.com), PBWorks (http://pbworks.com), Google Sites (http://sites .google.com), and Weebly (www.weebly.com) to type and post our work online, copying embed codes and uploading files within a web browser. We can share links to our own work, as well as the work of professionally produced websites or other "prosumers"—a term describing consumers who also produce content, made popular most recently by Donald Tapscott (see Tapscott 2008 and Tapscott and Williams 2006), through social networks such as Twitter (http://twitter.com) or, specifically for schools, Edmodo (www.edmodo.com).

Producing and publishing web-based text is as easy now as it has ever been—perhaps even more so with the advent of tools that allow us to create full websites straight from our mobile phones. Add to our alphabet soup of web abbreviations the likes of XML (Extensible Mark-up Language), CSS (Cascading Style Sheets), and RSS (Really Simple Syndication), and we have the ability to make our websites look different for various audiences and to "push" content into various apps that track what's happening online.

Notably, some genres *must* be created and viewed online. Hypertext fiction and transmedia storytelling require readers to participate with the text, some of which is alphabetic print and much of which is other media. For instance, the New York Times recently released a web-based, multimedia text, "Snow Fall: The Avalanche at Tunnel Creek," by John Branch (http://www.nytimes.com/projects/2012/ snow-fall/). It is beyond the scope of this book to go deeply into the crafting of such complex texts, although certainly important to note that these types of texts can be created with tools readily available for free online. Instead, I will focus on the types of texts we are likely to encounter in academic settings, including digital essays and learning journals. Nevertheless, the concluding case study shows some of the possibilities available to a digital writer today.

Web-based texts are more than just alphabetic text, and it is rare to find a website nowadays that doesn't have some form of interactive media beyond hyperlinks. Embedded media and advertisements are the main elements of web-based texts, although there may also be discussion forums, rollover links to other websites, and various other elements that distract from the main text. As Julie Coiro (2011) has described in relation to online reading comprehension, "[Readers'] level of metacognitive awareness about which strategies are best suited to locate, critically evaluate, and synthesize diverse online texts is likely to foster a deeper understanding of the texts they encounter on the Internet" (108). We need to be aware of this as digital writers, thinking carefully about the ways we compose texts for the web. The old adage of "reading like a writer, and writing for the reader" takes on a new twist. As Dana Wilber (2010) notes, students "are learning to create texts that are very different from the linear, written, paper-based text that schools depend on" (14). With that in mind, let's turn to a mentor text as a way to think about crafting this form of digital writing.

Viewing a Professional Mentor Text

There are literally billions of web pages we could choose when seeking mentor texts for our students. A place to start, perhaps, is to look at web pages that are not designed well, and this source site lives up to its name: www.webpagesthatsuck.com. Fortunately, the author, Vincent Flanders, offers a number of tips and examples of good design as well. Using a few examples from Flanders' "Top 30 Web Design Mistakes" (www.webpagesthatsuck.com/top-30-web-design-mistakes.html), we can identify then look at a mentor text. In choosing a mentor text for us to view, one you might use with students, I have gone to a reputable and engaging source: NASA. According to Flanders' tips, many of the elements of the NASA site (www.nasa.gov) get it right. Still, examine the NASA home page screenshot in Figure 3.1, taken in September 2012, then consider five of Flander's design mistakes:

Screenshot of NASA Home Page, September 2012

Figure 3.1

11. Quickly scanning the page doesn't tell our visitors much about its purpose.

17. We don't put design elements where our visitors expect them.

18. Logo is not on the top of every page and clicking it doesn't lead to the home page.

28. We don't know what content is popular.

30. The important content does not fit in the first screen.

How have the digital writers who crafted the NASA home page addressed these issues? Did they fall into the traps, or were they able to design a useful, aesthetically pleasing website?

NASA's logo, in the top-left corner, remains consistent across the linked pages, as do the buttons across the top and the links for the public, for educators, for students, and for media. The buttons—News, Missions, Multimedia, Contact, and About NASA—also reveal drop-down menus when the cursor hovers over. A search box is built into the top part of the page, with plenty of space surrounding it so a viewer can see it as a distinct feature. Even though it is packed with information, the page itself is not dense, and readers can get a general sense of the stories and sections through the thumbnail photos and cartoonlike logos on the right. Only one sans serif font is used for all the text, although headings are distinctly larger. All this content appears "above the fold," to use the old newspaper parlance, and there is even more detailed information below.

On the flip side, there are some drawbacks to the page design. While the colors are complementary and may evoke feelings of being in space, the black, gray, and blue combination does feel a bit drab. Given the wealth of information on the site, and the numerous links to access it, I wonder whether a user might go directly to the search feature rather than try to find what he was looking for using the main navigational menus. Finally, even when a reader finds the information he is looking for, multiple columns of information remain on the page, with plenty of links and potential distractions. While NASA has created a site where a wide variety of users would be able to access the rich content available, locating specific information could be difficult.

As a web-based mentor text, then, the NASA website offers us a way to talk with students about the textual and visual content, as well as the design choices. Recalling the MAPS heuristic, it is worth exploring the mode (an informational text), the media (a website with text, images, video, and links), as well as the multiple audiences and purposes the NASA website serves.

Considerations for Web Texts as Mentor Texts

In the early days of web publishing, most people were amazed by the information superhighway, the pure abundance of knowledge just one click away. Anyone could post anything. And it wasn't all aesthetically pleasing, let alone accurate. Nearly everyone—especially librarians and English teachers—also worried about credibility: who published this and for what purpose? Is the information accurate and reliable? Even if it looks good, can I trust this website?

While this is certainly still a consideration today (websites may be intended to be completely fictitious or carry a clear bias), most students who now search the web do so through what Eli Pariser (2011) calls "filter bubbles." In other words, when I do a Google search for a particular topic, as long as I am logged in under my user name, my results will be skewed based on my previous search history. Likewise, when I'm logged into Facebook and looking only at links my friends have sent me, my searching has been done for me and is similarly skewed. Pariser warns that the kinds of searches we do, and their results, could negatively influence our understanding of politics, religion, science, the arts, our communities, and ourselves.

Put more bluntly, Howard Rheingold, in his latest book, *Net Smart: How to Thrive Online* (2012), says we should be sure to verify questionable information with at least three other sources. He argues for five new literacies that will attune us to social media: attention, crap-detection, participation, collaboration, and network awareness. In essence, he wants us to pay attention to *how we pay attention*, especially when we are online. Before we share a link, make a comment, post a photo, or otherwise contribute something to the digital ether, we need to think about that action with intention. We need to think like digital writers: *Am I simply sharing a link to something that someone else crafted or offering my own succinct commentary on it? Am I composing my own response as a blog post, then sharing a link via Twitter? How much writing am I doing when I share something via social media? Am I intentional about it? Is this piece of my digital writing worth sharing?*

To that end, when students are looking for web-based mentor texts, we need to invite them to think clearly about both content and form. We want them to be able to differentiate, to use McLuhan's terms, between the medium and message, yet still understand the overall effect of both. While this is of course very difficult, and some websites are deliberately designed to lead the reader through in a particular manner, there are things we can keep in mind as we help students design websites, no matter what software they use—blogs, wikis, or any other type of website development tool.

When crafting any kind of digital writing, students should be reminded of the principles in Robin Williams' oft-cited *The Non-Designer's Design Book* (2008): contrast, repetition, alignment, and proximity. Sometimes called the CRAP principles, they can be summarized as follows:

- *Contrast*—If elements (colors, font, shapes, line, sizes) are not exactly the same, make them distinctly different in order to add visual interest to the page.

- *Repetition*—Some element should be repeated to provide a pattern within the piece.

- *Alignment*—Every element on a page should have a visual connection with other elements on the page to give an overall sense of order.

- *Proximity*—Group elements that are alike in terms of size, shape, or color, and put other elements at a distance.

Other elements to keep in mind that are specific to web-based texts include:

- Recognize that color schemes, backgrounds, fonts, and graphics may appear slightly different in different web browsers or devices.

- Integrate useful navigation links or buttons, and be aware of their placement on the page.

- Be judicious in the number and destination of internal and external links.

- Use media, including embedded images and videos, sensibly.

- Make a smart choice of designs from the gallery of templates (if applicable).

In thinking about the craft of writing web-based texts, I offer another way to categorize them: *digitally convenient* or *digitally enhanced*. Digitally convenient texts are essentially alphabetic texts posted online. Using tools such as blogs, wikis, collaborative word processors, or even social networks, a digital writer types a text (or more and more frequently these days, produces it using voice recognition software) and posts it online. These texts can remain private, be posted to a password-protected space, or be made available to the public. While the writing can be powerful and exhibit a strong voice, the texts are online only because we want students to have an audience or we want to assess their work easily. In other words, they don't *have* to be online, but it behooves us to have them posted to a blog or wiki, or shared via Google Docs, and allow opportunities to comment. These digitally convenient texts do not necessarily take advantage of any of the other features that make the web dynamic: hyperlinks, various fonts and color schemes, embedded media, RSS, or tags. There are good reasons for having students create digitally convenient texts, especially in the drafting stage when they are seeking feedback. But having students produce *only* digitally convenient texts shortchanges their opportunities as digital writers.

Alternatively, we can ask students to compose digitally enhanced web-based texts. These texts are not just alphabetic texts posted online; instead, they take advantage—or require—the use of hyperlinks, embedded media, and other features that make web-based texts dynamic. For example, a document could be presented online as a PDF (essentially an electronic version of the printed document, including special fonts, colors, and images) or as enhanced text on a website, with individual sections split into separate locations and external sources included as hyperlinks. The writing and design decisions necessary to produce a digitally enhanced text include elements of alphabetic text (what do I need to write here so that my audience understands my ideas?) as well as many choices about what else to include, such as links, images, videos, and other web-based elements. For instance, just because a writer could highlight a particular word and link it to an external definition, should she? Or, should she put the definition on another page of her website? Or include a short video that defines the word? One of the decisions with creating digitally enhanced texts is whether the text needs to be enhanced. Simply asking students to create a website and include a set number of links or images does not guarantee the text will be better—in fact, it could be worse, because the additional links or images could be superfluous and distracting.

Another advantage of creating web-based texts is that much of the formatting can be done behind the scenes, depending on the particular tool you (and your students) choose. The difficult work of hand-coding HTML and uploading files via FTP disappears when we use web-based services such as blogs, wikis, or website builders. This "improvement" is both good and bad, in that digital writers trade ease of use for customization: choices about design and layout are limited by the application, but having too many choices can be overwhelming, especially when one is first learning the technology. Still, writers should be conscious of the choices they are making, even when simply evaluating available templates (and noting that they can often tweak templates, too).

Curricular Connections

While the possibilities for putting digitally convenient texts online are nearly endless, my hope is that you invite your students to construct digitally enhanced texts such as those described in Table 3.1. At this point in each subsequent chapter, I will offer suggestions for using the three CCSS text types: narrative, informational, and argument.

Exploring the Digital Writing Process for Web Texts

In some ways, creating a web-based text is very similar to creating a print-based text. Authors brainstorm, develop ideas, scratch those ones, develop new ideas, and continually revise. The interesting difference between how those final ideas appear in print and as web-based text is that "transparency" becomes the online writing default. For instance, a blogger may focus on a particular issue over time, each entry offering a slightly different take. Unlike a journal, which sits in one person's desk or nightstand drawer, the blog becomes a public document, open for additional comment and easily searchable. Wikis, by their nature, are collaborative documents, welcoming groups large and small to compose shared documents that are easy to link and organize. Anyone can sign up for an account with a website-building service and have a functional site up and running in minutes. An overview of the composing process for web-based texts is presented in Table 3.2.

Table 3.1	Possibilities for Various Text Types with Different Web-Based Media		
Media	**Possibilities for Narrative Genres**	**Possibilities for Informational Genres**	**Possibilities for Argument Genres**
Blogs Blogger, WordPress, Tumblr	Serial novels, released a "chapter" at a time as individual posts	Topically focused blog, allowing for comments from readers and sharing links to authoritative sources	Dual-voiced blog in which two authors enter posts and comment on one another's ideas
Wikis Wikispaces, PBWorks	"Choose your own adventure" hyperlinks to different sections of the wiki or to descriptions of character, plot, etc.	Collaboratively constructed articles around a particular topic with embedded images and videos	Pages that maintain a "neutral point of view," a la Wikipedia, with accompanying discussion pages
Websites Google Sites, Weebly	Hypertext fiction that uses links to propel readers through the story	Topically focused sites on particular people, places, events, or ideas	"Debate" sites modeled after examples such as ProCon (http://procon.org)
Social Networks Twitter, Edmodo	Dialogues between existing or new characters, within a single text or across texts	Discussions focused on particular topics of expertise or interest	Debates between historical figures or modern personas on different sides of an issue

Prewriting and Drafting Web Texts

Depending on a writer's individual process, there are countless ways to gather and organize information for digital writing. Because students will be creating texts that are native to the web, it makes sense that the tools they use to compose them also function well in digital spaces. While there are countless other tools you might be able to use, and the website Cool Tools for Schools (http://cooltoolsforschools.wikispaces.com/) and its partner site, Cool Apps for Schools (http://coolappsforschools.wikispaces.com/), keep a pretty comprehensive list, I will mention a few here that are particularly useful for prewriting and drafting.

Table 3.2	Overview of the Composing Process for Web Text
Prewriting and Drafting	▪ Ideas are collected and shared with tools such as Diigo or Google Bookmarks (social bookmarking services) or Shelfster and Evernote (web clipping tools). ▪ Ideas are organized using mind-mapping tools such as Gliffy and Mindmodo. ▪ Sources are documented using citation tools such as Zotero, Citelighter, or EasyBib.
Revising and Editing	▪ Many web-based drafts are saved automatically, and revision history is easy to determine. ▪ Documents are edited collaboratively. ▪ Usage errors are checked using sites like Grammarly.
Publishing and Assessing	▪ Publication is instantaneous, and the text is accessible through any web browser or mobile device. ▪ The web-based texts are judged in relation to the criteria for effective digital writing.

Scan to view resources for *Crafting Digital Writing*.

(The companion wiki for this book includes an ever-growing list of websites and apps.)

Digital writing often requires viewing several websites at once, and many of the services listed below can be integrated as extensions with your web browser. You should know how to install add-ons or extensions and use tabbed browsing. If you are unfamiliar with these concepts, or any other concepts and tools in the book, I encourage you to search for a tutorial on YouTube. For instance, the search term *tabbed browsing tutorial* yields a number of useful videos for Safari, Firefox, Chrome, and Internet Explorer. Another popular source for tech-related tutorials is eHow Tech (www.ehow.com/ehow-tech/). Whatever way you search for tutorials, chances are someone has created a video that addresses many of your "how-to" questions.

Digital writers can collect and share ideas using social bookmarks such as Diigo (www.diigo.com) or Google Bookmarks (www.google.com/bookmarks) or web clipping tools such as Shelfster (http://shelfster.com/) and Evernote (http://evernote.com/). While each of these tools has its unique properties, they all help you keep track of information found on the web. Students who are just beginning the research process often say they "found something on Google/Yahoo/Bing." However, all information has a specific online home, and if you want to highlight a paragraph that is particularly relevant, these tools allow you to capture the text and save the URL for future citation.

Second, digital writers will want to organize their ideas. There are a number of ways to keep track of ideas and move them around, including simple lists in a word processor. There are also a number of mind-mapping tools such as Gliffy (www.gliffy.com/), Mindmodo (www.mindomo.com/), and even drawings in Google Docs (www.google.com/google-d-s/drawings/) that allow students to organize ideas graphically, create links between various diagrams, change fonts and colors, and otherwise conceptualize their information. Because students will be composing nonlinear web texts, accomplishing this kind of conceptual organizing in the planning stages is particularly important.

Finally, as students go back to the resources they have found previously and select the ones that will end up as citations, they can turn to online citation managers such as Zotero (www.zotero.org/), Citelighter (www.citelighter.com/), or EasyBib (www.easybib.com/). Again, each tool has unique features that appeal to varying grade levels; my guess is that Citelighter or EasyBib would be easiest for upper elementary and middle school students, and Zotero would be an invaluable resource for students in high school and college. Explore the help guides for each to make the right decision for your students.

Revising and Editing Web Texts

While revising and editing, students may choose not to make their work entirely public. This is certainly okay and can be used to the advantage of both the writer and the responder, whether another student or a teacher. Documents can be kept private, but still be open for collaborative editing. Many web-based drafts are saved automatically, and the revision history is easy to determine. Google Docs are saved every few seconds, and one can look at the detailed revision history at any time by clicking on the File menu. Many blogs and wikis also have automatic saving features that capture changes without the user's having to hit the Save button. Sites like Grammarly (www.grammarly.com/) can check for common usage errors. During this stage, digital writers will also make design decisions about color schemes, embedded media, and links.

TECH TIP: HOW TO EMBED MEDIA ELEMENTS

Most artifacts on a web-based online display service (YouTube, Flickr, Prezi, for example) can be "embedded" within a blog, wiki, or website. Sometimes the code you need to embed is evident as you look at the artifact; sometimes you need to click on a link. The YouTube code looks like the screenshot in Figure 3.2. It allows you to paste this particular YouTube video, in video player format, to any webpage. The <iframe> commands tell how wide and high video player will appear; underneath is the link to the video. Knowing how to embed images, video, and other media elements from outside web sources is one way to keep your own website's storage space from getting clogged up with tons of media files as well as a way to acknowledge the original source so people can easily link to it.

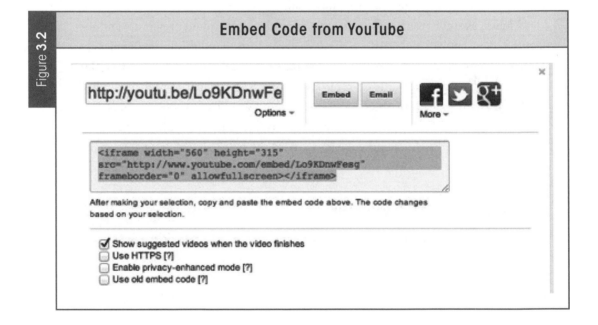

Figure 3.2

Embed Code from YouTube

Publishing Web Texts

Finally, we get to publication. Many options are available. Will students post their content to an internal space within the school or district? Will they post their work to a third-party space that is still private? Will they post online for the world to see? It would be too lengthy an exercise to walk through the steps, let alone the benefits and constraints, of publishing in any or all these spaces. The pertinent aspects will become clear as you explore the various options with many of the web-based services listed in Appendix B. That said, helping students see real audiences and purposes for their work often means moving beyond school boundaries, and I encourage you to make that move with your students to the broader networks these web-based tools allow us to connect with.

Also, as more colleges and companies look to discover a student's web presence before offering them a position, creating a smart, thoughtful digital footprint is an invaluable life skill. As I described in *The Digital Writing Workshop*, inviting students to create a digital portfolio is an easy way for you as their teacher to keep track of what your students have been doing. Helping students understand how they are building their digital footprint is incredibly important, and being able to gather their best digital work in one online space will become increasingly useful as they prepare for college and career. Any of the digital writing products they create have the opportunity to be shared, helping them establish themselves online. In the final chapter, we will look at a collection of work from one student, Lydia, as well as a digital portfolio compiled by my son, Tyler.

TECH TIP: MOZILLA'S HACKASAURUS

Now that your students know how to create websites, help them understand how to hack them. Using the basic code to change hyperlinks or embed different types of images, students can "hack" current websites with Mozilla's free tool, Hackasaurus (http://hackasaurus.org/). As the Hackasaurus site states:

> *Hackasaurus spreads skills, attitudes, and ethics that help youth thrive in a remixable digital world. By making it easy for youth to tinker and mess around with the building blocks that make up the web, Hackasaurus helps tweens move from digital consumers to active producers, seeing the web as something they can actively shape, remix and make better.*

Understanding that web texts, like all texts, are constructed by people with particular ideas and agendas is an incredibly important aspect of students' skills as web producers. Helping them understand the components of websites that they take for granted, such as the tags that indicate a heading, hyperlink, or image, can help them better understand website design and how different elements appear in different web browsers or on mobile devices. Playing with Hackasuarus allows them to make these changes although it does not change the original website, just the way it appears in your browser.

For instance, Figure 3.3 is a sample "hack" of Heinemann's website that I created. Inviting students to understand how websites are created, using tools like Hackasaurus, helps them think about their own content and design. It can also move quickly into a lesson on media literacy, and be a chance for students to simply have some fun remixing different components of websites. How might your students "hack" existing sites, using them as examples for understanding critical media literacy?

An Example of a "Hacked" Website Image

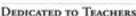

Figure 3.3

Assessing Web Texts

When we assess web texts we are looking not only for traditional qualities of writing such as clear sentences, enough detail, and an overall sense of organization but also for elements that make a web-based text truly digitally enhanced. In other words, we are assessing both the quality of the writing and also whether the author has truly taken advantage of the technology by using hyperlinks, embedding multimedia, and organizing the text in a visually appealing manner.

One way to evaluate a website is to have students critique their own work using one of the many website evaluation guides produced by libraries. The four components of website credibility in the University of Maryland Libraries guide are particularly useful for evaluating the craft of digital writing and whether readers will be able to use and enjoy it.

- Assess *authority and accuracy* with questions such as, *Does the website provide a means of communicating with the author or webmaster?*

- Assess *purpose and content* with questions such as, *Is the point of view presented in a direct manner, or is it presented in an unbalanced and unreasonable way? Are arguments well supported?*

- Assess *currency* with questions such as, *Is the site well maintained? Are links current and working or do they lead to outdated pages and/or error messages?*

- Assess *design, organization, and ease of use* with questions such as, *Is the website clearly organized, easy to read, use and navigate?*

(University of Maryland Libraries 2011)

Put another way, Coiro's (2011) "metacognitive awareness" strategies for Internet readers also apply to those writers who create web-based texts. If we hold to the adage that "good readers are the best writers," then our students' understanding of how to critically evaluate web-based texts will serve them well as they begin to compose their own.

Examples of Student-Composed Web Texts

Many overlapping decisions go into the craft of composing digitally enhanced web-based texts, so let's now examine how some student writers have gone about this process. The first example is a creative nonfiction piece titled "A Special Kind of Smile" that Nicole, a middle school student, crafted with Google Docs. Nicole combines a personal narrative about a rare form of dental disease with information about the condition, *Amelogenesis imperfecta*. The second example is a pair of high school essays analyzing Arthur Miller's *Death of a Salesman*. "Untitled" was composed with Google Docs, "The Plight of the Common Man" on a wiki; both employ images and links that make them digital essays. The final example is an elementary school science journal composed on a wiki over the course of three months. We'll analyze these examples on the basis of the MAPS heuristic students used to guide their process.

Example 1: A Special Kind of Smile

Scan to view
Nicole's essay.

"Today is the day i go to Ann Arbor for the first time."

So begins a creative nonfiction piece by eighth-grader Nicole Waugh that blends personal narrative, informational research, and various features of Google Docs to create an engaging digitally enhanced text. Penny Lew, a middle school teacher in Farwell, Michigan, invites her students to compose multigenre projects about topics of personal interest, employing creative writing and good research skills in doing so. She also invites them to create wiki-based portfolios of their work (http://mslew.wikispaces.com/). In this essay, Nicole describes her experience with a painful dental disorder, *Amelogenesis imperfecta*: http://goo.gl/99Ji1.

Reading this first sentence of Nicole's essay, you could reach for your red pen to correct the capitalization error (although you would have to mark the text digitally), and no doubt other errors occur throughout the text that can affect the meaning Nicole is trying to convey. However, I urge you to look past the minor surface errors and see what Nicole has accomplished in her essay. You can see some of the features in the screenshot in Figure 3.4, but I encourage you to go to the wiki page and view the work in its entirety before reading my analysis below.

To begin, we see Nicole has worked to make her text visually distinct by choosing different font faces and colors. In the title, she seems to be experimenting with all the colors of the rainbow. In the first section, she recalls driving to Ann Arbor from her home in northern Michigan and entering the dentist's office. Again, while there are certainly some concerns here about the way that the time, and subsequently the verb tense, shifts from a reflection into the current moment, it is clear that Nicole is trying to describe her experience, even incorporating some sentence variety ("Then i realize i stopped breathing. I went stiff and tried to keep my eyes from watering because i was so scared."). Before she changes perspective by switching to a new font face and color, as well as by creating a diary entry, she includes a link to a separate slide show (see the cover slide in Figure 3.5). By inserting this as a hyperlink, she gives the reader the option to view the slide show at the present moment or come back and click on it later. In my first reading, I chose to click on the link so I could better understand why she might have included it there.

> ## Introduction to "A Special Kind of Smile"
>
> Figure 3.4
>
> ### A Speci l Kind of Smile
>
> Today is the day i go to Ann Arbor for the first time. I am so nervous because I have no idea what they are going to do. We are on the highway and I am up front. I am being more quiet than usual and my brother is in the back blabbing away. The only thing i am looking forward to is my teeth not being yellow and crooked. Questions are running through my mind taking up all my thoughts. What if they can't fix it? What are they going to do? Am i going to feel anything? As this is all running through my mind, we pull up to the dentistry school. Then i realize i stopped breathing. I went stiff and tried to keep my eyes from watering because i was so scared. We pulled into the parking lot, and my mom said, "well, we're here." We got out of the van, walked to the front doors and went inside. The moment we got to the pediatric dentist i can hear younger kids crying and screaming. My mom checked my brother and I in, then we sat down waiting for our names to be called. My brother was first then about 20 minutes later my name was called. I walked over and went with the lady. She sat me in a chair and told me what she was going to do, suddenly i wasn't so scared anymore.
>
> Slide Show
>
> Day 1, So today i went to the dentist. But, it wasn't just a normal dentist visit... turns out i need all my teeth capped. They said it shouldn't hurt too much but i'm not so sure. What i don't get is why my brother isn't getting the same thing done.

In the slide show, Nicole leads the reader through a more detailed description of her condition, beginning with a slide titled "What Is Amelogenesis Imperfecta?" Blending some of her personal experience with a more scientific explanation of the condition, the four remaining slides describe how Amelogenesis Imperfecta (AI) can be corrected cosmetically, how it affects Nicole emotionally, and how rare the condition is. She uses a personal tone, yet includes facts; for example, "In my description it is a hereditary condition resulting in a yellow or brownish color to the teeth." Including the slide show at this point in the essay gives the reader a chance to understand a bit more about AI and why Nicole is nervous about her trip. While the hyperlink "Slide Show" could have been more descriptive or embedded in the paragraph, the fact that Nicole recognized how this information best served the

Figure 3.5

Cover Slide for "A Smile to Remember: Things I Have Learned"

A Smile to Remember

Things I Have Learned

[x-ray of teeth]

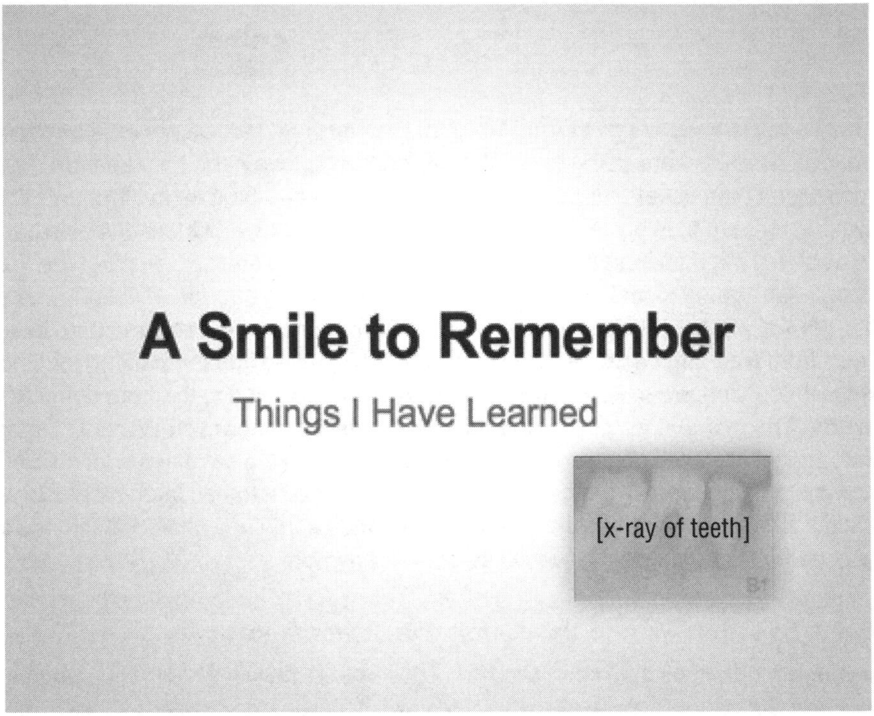

Just a quick reminder: in this piece of student work and in others in this chapter, we have replaced images that the student used with a description of the images. While it is considered fair use for students to use copyrighted images for educational purposes, it is not fair use to print them in a book that is being offered for sale. For more information about fair use and copyright law, see page 9 of the introduction.

reader as a link outside the text shows that she understands this element of craft in digital writing.

The diary entry begins with the designation *Day 1* and then discusses what the dentist has prescribed for her in terms of treatment and compares her own condition with that of her brother. Scrolling quickly through the rest of the text, the reader sees three other diary entries; one is marked *Day 2*, another *Day 14*, and the final one has a calendar date. This parallels the passing of time in the narrative. The informational text about her condition is interspersed with the diary entries related to her treatment and the feeling she is experiencing; as a reader, I wonder whether she intentionally chose the color blue to represent sadness.

Beneath the diary entry for day 1, Nicole makes an interesting move, adopting the voices of the teeth. Building on the tradition of craft as charted by authors like

> ## Third Section—"The Life of a Not Normal Tooth (in script form)"
>
> Figure 3.6
>
> **Day 1, So today i went to the dentist. But, it wasn't just a normal dentist visit... turns out i need all my teeth capped. They said it shouldn't hurt too much but i'm not so sure. What i don't get is why my brother isn't getting the same thing done.**
>
> ### The Life Of a Not Normal Tooth
> ### *(in script form)*
>
> Tooth #1 "Yaaayyy!!! we get to go to the dentist today and get
> Tooth #2 " Umm not really, do you know how much that hurts?"
> Tooth #3 " Yeah, whenever that one person squirts us with water, I try to cover myself"
> Tooth #1 "Oh yeah... i forgot about that part..."
> Tooth #4 "FORGOT? HOW DO YOU FORGET SOMETHING THAT PAINFUL?"
> Tooth #1 " I don't know i just did! I have a short memory okay!"
>   *All teeth turn to Tooth #5 A.K.A "the wisdom tooth or wise tooth"*
> All teeth "Wise tooth, why don't you ever complain?"
> Wise Tooth "because i have a cap on, so I don't feel as much." [clip art of cartoon teeth]
> Tooth #1 "what's that?"
> Wise Tooth " something that covers us to keep us safe, and things don't hurt us as much"
> Tooth #1 "oh, doesn't it hurt to get those things on?"
> Wise tooth "only for a little bit. Then you start to relax"
>
> **Day 2; So I am going back to the dentist in 2 weeks to start the work. I am really nervous... my dad said he would see if he could go with... he probably won't.**

[clip art of cartoon teeth]

[clip art of cartoon teeth]

Barry Lane, who encourages us to take on different personas, this short dialogue involves five different teeth talking about the experience of going to be cleaned. Of course, Nicole is describing her own experience with AI, in that Tooth 1 is excited to go for the cleaning and yet the other three teeth remind it about the pain they will soon experience. There are at least three craft elements that I find interesting here:

- She chooses green text and a format similar to how characters' lines are written in a play.

- She uses clip art of teeth to indicate different characters (although not all five).

- She shifts to ALL CAPS (an indication of yelling in online discussion forums, chat rooms, and emails) when Tooth 4 exclaims: "FORGOT? HOW DO YOU FORGET SOMETHING THAT PAINFUL?"

Figure 3.7

"About My Case of Amelogenesis Imperfecta"

About my Case of Amelogenesis Imperfecta

- Under my caps my teeth are yellow.
- Without braces, my teeth would be really crooked.
- I might need surgery.
- Not very many people have it.
- I have an open bite because of my short teeth.
- Cold things hurt my teeth.
- I will have it my whole life.
- Its really hard to keep my teeth clean.
- I think it's stupid having to explain what i have every time someone makes fun of me.
- I have been sick and tired of it since kindergarten.
- I have an open bite.

Day 14: well tomorrow is the day i will go to Ann Arbor to start all my dental work. We have to get up around 4:30am to make it there by 8:00. My mom is always telling me that it won't hurt... but I'm not so sure...

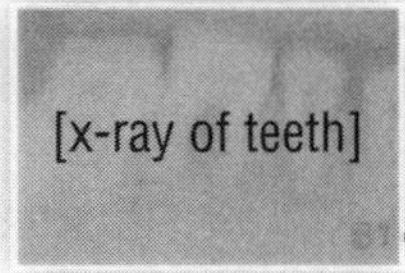

[x-ray of teeth]

This is an X-ray of what peoples teeth look like with A.I. All crooked, squished together and quite short.

By adopting the persona of different teeth, including the "Wise Tooth" who tells the reader about the cap that protects it, she is able to tell her own story of coming to understand what dentistry will need to take place in order for her to feel better.

In the fourth section, Nicole shifts back to blue for the diary-like description; in the fifth section, she describes a second trip to Ann Arbor. Then she makes another interesting shift in voice for the sixth section, "About My Case of Amelogenesis Imperfecta." Along with listing the facts of her particular case, which were elaborated in the slide show, she now includes a bulleted list of eleven elements specific to her case. The first eight are very clinical, with examples such as "Under my caps my teeth are yellow" and "Cold things hurt my teeth." The final three items are two very personal emotional responses—"I think it's stupid having to explain what i have every time someone makes fun of me" and "I have been sick and tired of it since kindergarten"—followed at the very end with "I have an open bite." It is clear in this list that Nicole understands her medical condition and at the same time sees it as a part of her identity. Again, while we could look at this list and say she needed to stick with the medical facts—she could elaborate on the emotional aspects in other sections of the piece—the nonlinearity of digital writing comes through here. Bullet points are usually included in technical reports, not emotional statements, yet there is something powerful about seeing them combined here.

The seventh section jumps ahead to day 14, again showing how time is passing during her treatment. In an informational text, a more direct transition with the use of a subheading might need to be included. However with this multigenre approach within a singular piece of writing, Nicole is able to show how she continues to react to her treatment while also discussing it in a scientific manner. In the eighth section, she includes the sample image of a tooth, the same image from her slide show. This is a harbinger of what will come later in her essay, which includes multiple pictures of dentistry equipment. However, it is also an interesting moment to reflect on the craft of digital writing and how she could have saved the link for her slide show until later. What if this image had been the embedded link to the slide show? Readers, after understanding some of the scientific and emotional ramifications of her condition, could have been linked to more information.

Moving forward, section nine reintroduces the reflective journal, followed by a series of captioned pictures including the "rubber dam," a "numb shot," and "caps." These images were obviously found online, most likely through an image search. This raises some interesting questions about how Nicole could have crafted this particular section of her essay. I'm not sure whether she and her parents have a mobile phone with a digital camera or a regular digital camera, but it's interesting to speculate that Nicole could have documented her experience by taking her own pictures rather than simply finding some online. This is a question of craft and intention; if a digital writer is going to create a multimodal essay like this, knowing that images will play a key role in the composition, to what extent should we as teachers request or even demand that she take her own pictures? Part of this, of course, is the ever present element of time. Perhaps Nicole had only a few days between dentist visits to put together this essay, and taking those pictures would have been impossible. However, if she'd had enough time and had developed the topic with forethought, Nicole could have taken pictures of her actual visit. This would

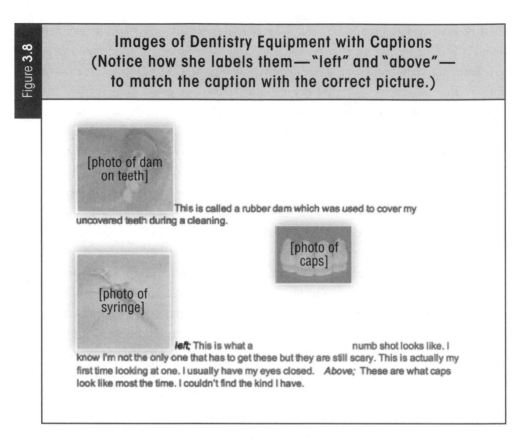

Figure 3.8

**Images of Dentistry Equipment with Captions
(Notice how she labels them—"left" and "above"—
to match the caption with the correct picture.)**

[photo of dam on teeth]

This is called a rubber dam which was used to cover my uncovered teeth during a cleaning.

[photo of caps]

[photo of syringe]

left: This is what a numb shot looks like. I know I'm not the only one that has to get these but they are still scary. This is actually my first time looking at one. I usually have my eyes closed.   *Above:* These are what caps look like most the time. I couldn't find the kind I have.

make the piece both more personal and (even though the likely copyrighted found images are being employed within fair use) not subject to copyright restrictions, since the images would be her own.

One of the criticisms that could be made of this piece of writing—despite the effective touches like the changes in the writer's voice, as well as in the fonts and colors—is that it really lacks a conclusion: "The End" is ineffective. However, in some ways, it makes sense. Journals or diaries continue, and Nicole has taken a summary/response approach, as well as provided day-to-day documentation of her dental work. Web pages that are crafted for informational purposes (as sections of her text clearly have been) aren't necessarily constructed with a beginning, a middle, and an end, so she must signal an ending somehow. She employs a great deal of dental vocabulary such as "ultrasonic cleaning" and "full mouth debridement." Finally, there is the addition of the slide show, a link that extends our understanding of AI as well as of the feelings Nicole has toward her condition. So, while "The

End" may not be the most effective conclusion, in her mind it might have been better than simply letting the text end the page.

In summary, this digitally enhanced essay shows how Nicole is developing as a digital writer. Considering the mode and media—while some of her uses of colors and fonts could be seen as gratuitous, and some elements of the overall layout could be aligned and improved—she has crafted a multigenre piece that documents her experience using medical vocabulary, her own anxieties about her condition, and hints about other tensions in her life. She conveys an effective message to her audience about this rare, yet serious condition. In some ways, the Google Doc limits her ability to design a more robust digital composition, which might have been even more engaging as a website with multiple pages, some focused on the narrative about her experience and others focused on the information about AI. In a more positive light, limiting some of those additional choices probably helped Nicole stay focused on the task at hand and get more alphabetic text written in the process.

Example 2: Death of a Salesman Essays

In her senior AP English class, Beth Nelson, a teacher at Greenville High School, in Michigan, built on an idea originally presented by Jim Burke on his English Companion Ning. In "The Digital Essay" (Burke 2011), he describes how to include the digital options in the essay.

> *Incorporate into your paper, where appropriate, hot links, images, video, or graphics. These should be incorporated into the paper, not tacked on or serving no evident purpose other than satisfying the requirements of this assignment.*

Burke goes on to describe two kinds of links.

> *"Required" links take the reader to information/content that is necessary to understand what they have not yet read; "optional" links offer additional or background information for those unfamiliar with the subject. Be mindful of which type you are including and write your sentence so as to make it clear how the reader should respond.*

Writers are encouraged to create essays that go beyond being digitally convenient (posted online) to being digitally enhanced (employing multimedia in smart ways). Links and images should not be gratuitous.

In Beth's class, students were crafting responses to Arthur Miller's classic, *Death of a Salesman* (Miller 1998). She asked them to create essays based on the criteria in Burke's original assignment. Represented here are two essays, "The Plight of the Common Man," by Alexandra Wagner (http://goo.gl/Ar1Nk), and "Untitled," by Makayla Larabell. There are similarities in the essays—which should be expected, given the static criteria as well as the expectations of senior writers in an AP English classroom—as well as some telling differences in the craft decisions these digital writers each made.

Scan to view
Alexandra's essay.

Scan to view
Makayla's essay.

In the first essay, Alexandra crafts a traditional persuasive piece, laying out her thesis at the end of the first paragraph: "Miller used the mental and physical death and ungluing of Willy to depict how a capitalistic society and how the disillusionment of the American Dream affects the dignity and choices of the common man." (See Figure 3.9.) Yet, even before she gets to this thesis, she is already crafting her digital essay to capture the reader's attention, provide context, and highlight the points she wants to make. She situates her title between two iconic images from the play, and within the first sentence has already created links for readers to explore. While visiting Arthur Miller's page on Wikipedia or viewing an extra video could be considered distracting, they also represent a type of prereading, offering us the chance to get some background information so that we will be better able to comprehend the essay.

The video she links to is a montage of clips from the filmed version of the Broadway production of the play starring Dustin Hoffman. Called "Death of a Salesman Trailer," its title on YouTube, the video was posted by willyloman1985. The clips relate to the title of the short film ("The Dramatic Life of Willy Loman") and are all Hoffman/Loman one-liners, carefully edited into a minute-and-a-half montage. Given that this is the second link in her digital essay, if I as a reader choose to go to this video, I will be distracted from my reading of the essay for less than two minutes, and the comic nature of the film sets the tone in my mind for the character of Willy Loman as I read the rest of Alexandra's analysis.

Throughout the remainder of the essay, Alexandra examines many of the metaphors in the play, offering links to a variety of images and definitions. Her essay engages the reader with its design and layout, including links and images that

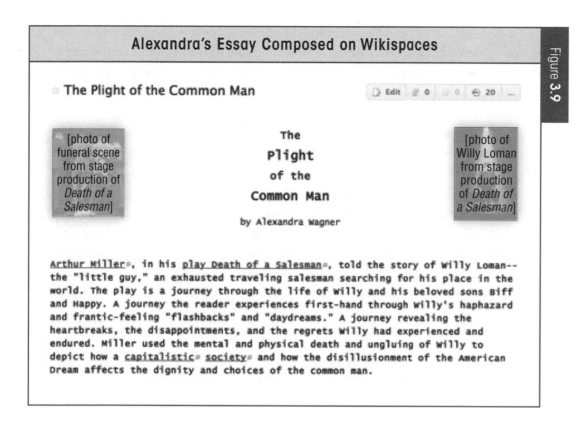

Alexandra's Essay Composed on Wikispaces

Figure 3.9

☆ **The Plight of the Common Man**   ⟨ Edit   ✎ 0   ⤓ 0   ⊖ 20   ...

[photo of funeral scene from stage production of *Death of a Salesman*]

The
Plight
of the
Common Man

by Alexandra Wagner

[photo of Willy Loman from stage production of *Death of a Salesman*]

Arthur Miller⌐, in his play Death of a Salesman⌐, told the story of Willy Loman-- the "little guy," an exhausted traveling salesman searching for his place in the world. The play is a journey through the life of Willy and his beloved sons Biff and Happy. A journey the reader experiences first-hand through Willy's haphazard and frantic-feeling "flashbacks" and "daydreams." A journey revealing the heartbreaks, the disappointments, and the regrets Willy had experienced and endured. Miller used the mental and physical death and ungluing of Willy to depict how a capitalistic⌐ society⌐ and how the disillusionment of the American Dream affects the dignity and choices of the common man.

support rather than detract from the argument she is attempting to make. She does not use an image of Arthur Miller at the top of the page, nor does she employ clip art. Using images from the film and the original theatrical production, she introduces us to the characters of the book. She also uses the image of a city and the pencil drawing of Loman pounding the ground. The images she chooses are black and white, or at least lack lots of color, so that the focus remains on the stark contrast between Loman's experience and what he perceives to be the American Dream.

These links and images enhance the text because readers can still understand the meaning Alexandra intends without clicking on them, yet a click will bring a deeper, more nuanced reading. She has made an important craft decision by not including these definitions or extraneous images in the essay, allowing the reader to explore them only if necessary. The images she does include in the essay complement rather than detract from the reading experience. While not the main focus of her essay, Alexandra is able to criticize American capitalism and greed through links to additional readings. Her conclusion, "The slow deconstruction of Willy's mental and physical health eventually led to his death—the final and most dramatic representation of the effects of capitalism on a man that could no longer provide for his family, a man that was too common—too 'low'—to achieve his dreams," is accentuated with the pencil sketch of Loman pounding on the floor.

In the second essay (the first screenshot is shown in Figure 3.10), Makayla begins to develop the thesis that using tools is important, and to some extent she keeps this theme throughout, both in images and in words. For instance, she quotes Loman, who says a "man who can't handle tools is not a man," and then brings in additional examples about rebuilding his house and the dream of building a guest house. She does include two links to an online version of the book, citing specific page numbers for particular quotes. In the second sentence, the word *play* is a link to a video, also called "Death of a Salesman Trailer," its YouTube title, which is described by its creator, Konamakona, as "A simple trailer that i made for an English

Figure 3.10

Makayla's Essay Composed on a Google Docs

Working with tools and building things is one motif that is repeatedly mentioned in the play Death of a Salesman, by Arthur Miller. The entire play is about Willy Loman's struggle as a common man with the American Dream and his own personal dreams which is to work with his hands.

[photo of Arthur Miller]

[photo of Charley from stage production of *Death of a Salesman*]

What Willy says and what he does are two different things. He talks about his true dream, but he follows the American Dream, and society's standards.

[stock photo of a smiling family outside their home]

During a game of cards with Charley, Willy reveals what he believes a true man is and he tells Charley, "A man who can't handle tools is not a man." (1888) Willy believes a true man can work with tools and fix things, and that is what Willy loves to do, and that is his true destiny. Throughout the project." The video shows the complicated relationship Loman has with his sons and wife, pulling out key scenes from the film showing their conflicts.

Throughout the essay, Makayla uses images of Arthur Miller, an actor playing Willy Loman, a modern family, a poster advertising the play, stock photos of construction workers, and a clip art drawing of a father and son building something together. In her conclusion, she mentions "the motif of working with tools and building things," yet much of her essay is about Loman's desire to be "well liked." This montage of images and themes in the essay itself make for a somewhat confusing reading experience. Is the essay about Arthur Miller? Do the particular images of the play poster or of Willy Loman articulate the points Makayla is trying to make better than the stock photos and clip art? Would she have been better served to stick with the main theme of using tools and include the information about being "well liked" on a separate page? Unlike Alexandra's essay, which uses internal links to elaborate on some of the ideas as well as external links to sources she is citing, Makayla highlights large sections of text and links to the sources for support, forcing the reader to gain a much better sense of what she is saying by finding out what others are saying.

Given the argumentative mode, as well as the web-based media, the two essays have a number of similarities, and both writers make strong attempts to integrate images and links that are definitely digitally enhanced. In other words, mode and media matter; a reader's understanding of the essays would not be the same without the images and links. (Even if they are not employed as skillfully as they could be, each writer attempts a rhetorical use.) Even more telling is the way these two students employ the craft of digital writing to meet the purpose of accentuating their arguments as well as to make their essays aesthetically pleasing.

A closer analysis of these two essays shows how their authors made craft decisions as digital writers, fulfilling Burke's request that students "incorporate into your paper, where appropriate, hot links, images, video, or graphics." Table 3.3 summarizes the digital writing decisions Alexandra and Makayla made.

First, I include word count because it seems important that Alexandra's essay is nearly twice as long. (This count does not include a separate "Works Cited" page.) Of course, digital texts can be as long as they need to be without fear of taking up too much paper. Still, word counts are one measure of a writer's output.

Next, it is interesting that each essay contains six embedded images, although each writer uses these images in slightly different ways. Alexandra includes four

Table 3.3	Comparison of Alexandra's and Makayla's Composing Choices									
	Total words	Total linked words	Images related to the play	Additional images	Internal links	External links	Links to videos	Links to pictures	Academic sources cited	Other external sources
Alexandra	1011	34 (3%)	4	2	3	6	1	4	12	4
Makayla	624	51 (8%)	3	3	0	10	1	0	10	8

images related to the play, but no image of Miller. Makayla uses three images related to the play and one image of Miller; the other images are from stock art.

Regarding total links within the essays, both writers employ about the same number of links (fourteen and eleven), but looking at them as a ratio to overall word count, a startling difference appears. Even though Makayla's essay contains eighteen sources, two of them—the Wikipedia entry and the online version of the text—are repeated. Alexandria uses a total of fourteen links in thirty-four words, so a total of just over 3 percent of her text is linked to outside sources. Makayla links fifty-one words, so her overall percentage of links to text is just over 8 percent. How the writers employed the links is also important. Alexandra's links are along the lines of what Burke would describe as "required," whereas Makayla's links, especially to the online version of the text without any analysis, are what I would classify as "optional."

We should also note the difference between the two video trailers that the writers chose to link to; Alexandra cites an "official" movie trailer from the studio, while Makayla cites a trailer that was "remixed" from original footage. What does this say about their supporting evidence, as well as their ability to use multimedia effectively in their research? In some ways, a remixed trailer might offer greater support for an author's point, especially if that point is sarcasm or parody. However, given that these essays were crafted for an academic audience, I wonder how effective either writer was in searching for the right kind of supporting video evidence or incorporating the link into the essay.

In summary, then, the writing in each essay has strengths and weaknesses, and each writer employs media (including the links and embedded pictures) in a different way. As a teacher, I would think about how to judge the quality of the writing in conjunction with how well the writers integrated the digital elements. Are these essays digitally convenient, or are they digitally enhanced? What questions might we ask Alexandra and Makayla to help them use the digital features to the best of their ability and make their writing more effective? How did the situation presented by their assignment both empower and constrain them as writers?

Example 3: Wiki-Based Science Journals

This final example of a student's web-based text comes from classroom of Tim Saunders, a teacher in Grand Rapids, Michigan. As part of his unit on matter, Tim took a game theory approach, inviting his students to form guilds and embark on a "quest." Part of the quest was to document their learning through a wiki page. Although public web access to these examples is not available, I received permission from one of Tim's students and her parents, fourth-grader Gracie Gorsline, to use sceenshots from her online journal.

On the initial screen, shown in Figure 3.11, we see that Gracie and her teammates have made a combined total of sixty-nine revisions (noted by a small clock in the editing toolbar in the upper-right area). Clicking on the clock icon reveals that this journal was constructed over the course of three months, from February to April, during an extensive unit on the study of matter. The edit toolbar also indicates that there were five discussion posts. These were simple conversations between Gracie and her teammates, more social than academic. (This social element is inherent in digital writing tools and, to the extent that the social interactions help build collaboration and trust, very useful.) "Level 1" under the guild name tells us this is the first set of data collected in their series of quests.

Gracie and her teammates added different types of content over the course of the unit. For example, in two points on the wiki page Tim had groups record a podcast to summarize the work they had done in that portion of the quest; for the other portions, they composed a brief summary. Also, as we see in the screenshot in Figure 3.12, Tim had them take pictures of their work in progress—of both the experiment and their notes. During the three-month unit, Gracie's group produced nearly 3,000 words, took twelve pictures, and entered numerous data points that compared and contrasted changes in matter over time.

Figure 3.11

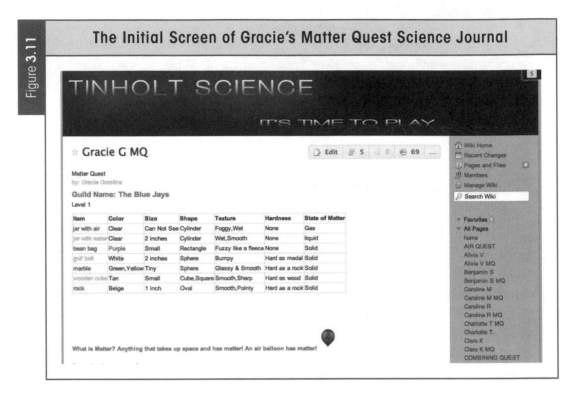

The Initial Screen of Gracie's Matter Quest Science Journal

The CCSS calls for more literacy activities across the curriculum, and a wiki-based journal of a scientific experiment is one way students can use digital writing tools to document their learning. A blog or a Google Doc may work just as well. The point is that each student is able to document the work as part of the team—adding comments, making suggestions, and sharing media such as podcasts—while maintaining his or her own wiki page. Tharp (2010) explains the advantages of wikis as follows:

> *The wiki format allows teachers to provide ongoing response to assess student performance in conjunction with peer-to-peer evaluations, self-reflections, and holistic scoring guidelines. The essential nature of a wiki is to allow students to take an active role in composing while teaching them to work together to compose, revise, and edit an end product. (41)*

This web-based text was available to individual students as well as the class, and Tim was able to share examples of strong writing by clicking on a link and pulling

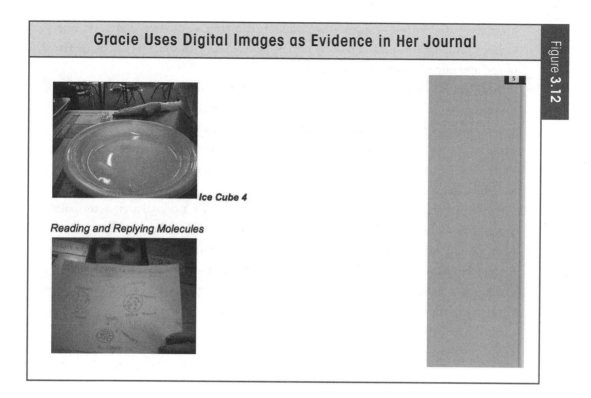

it up on screen as a mentor text. Returning to the MAPS elements one final time this chapter, I find it important to note that the situation for this writing—informal, but extensive—offers students a different purpose for using the wiki than the digital essays shown above. Rather than displaying a final product, Gracie's wiki page serves as a way for her to track her thinking over time and includes a variety of types of evidence that she gathered, not just links to other sites.

Conclusion

The kinds of web-based texts students can now produce with their computers, phones, tablets, digital cameras, and other Internet-connected devices are both daunting and exhilarating. Students truly have the opportunity to make their voices heard around the world. The examples in this chapter—digital essays and science journals—are but two of many ways students can craft web-based digital writing. Other examples are opinion pieces, stories, poetry, informational websites, debate blogs, and any of a number of other genres.

However, we need to make sure that our *students* are producing these texts—that the writing is their own critical thinking, and not always a link to the work of others. It's easy to find something cool on the Internet and post a link to it as a status update, essentially saying *wow, look at this!* And, of course, we want them to cite their sources and build on the ideas of others. Yet, it's something else entirely to use the discovered information to create your own original content, developing something uniquely your own. While technology allows a digital writer to make hyperlinks—and the assigned writing task may demand links be included—these links should still be purposeful. Web-based texts require a number of skills from digital writers, including a clear attention to organization and aesthetics, as well as making good decisions about how to present one's own content, a focus we will continue to explore in the next chapter on presentations.

CRAFTING PRESENTATIONS

Every decision a designer makes is intentional. Reason and logic underpin the placement of visual elements. Meaning underscores the order and hierarchy of ideas.

(Duarte 2008, 83)

For many years now, the ubiquitous practice of having students present a slide show in front of the class has been one of the chief complaints by those railing against educational technology. Often mind-numbing, the reality that students barely do any research below the surface, then copy and paste big chunks of text and images onto a series of preformatted slides and regurgitate them in front of a class of their bored peers should make any educator angry. However, that does not mean we should give up asking our students to craft effective digital writing in the form of presentations. We just need to teach them effective craft.

Now more than ever the options for creating web-based presentations allow students the kind of variety they need to both differentiate instruction and employ a variety of multimedia sources. There is no excuse for "power pointless" presentations. Instead, students have endless opportunities to prepare presentations for both real-time and on-demand delivery. Helping students understand how to best use text, images, video, music, and other media to effectively deliver their message is a key component of the speaking and listening skills in the Common Core Standards.

As with all forms of digital writing, the secret to effective presentations is an intentional focus on craft. Relying again on Robin Williams' core principles of contrast, repetition, alignment, and proximity, we can help students begin visualizing their presentations in more effective ways. The MAPS heuristic also helps them understand when and how to deliver an effective presentation to a variety of audiences, especially noting that these presentations will likely need to engage their peers as well as the adults that will be evaluating their work.

Books related to presentations in the corporate world—including those by Guy Kawasaki, Garr Reynolds, and Nancy Duarte—make it clear that good presentations are a matter of more than selling a product or making an argument. At least two other factors are at work: "stickiness" (the ability of your presentation's message to make a lasting impression) and storytelling. For those of us who teach writing and for all of us who enjoy stories, the storytelling factor is obvious: you're not simply marketing a new product but positioning viewers in a story of how the product relates to them. The other factor, "stickiness," is a bit more intangible. On his blog, *Presentation Zen*, Reynolds (2007) summarizes six principles from Chip and Dan Heath's book *Made to Stick: Why Some Ideas Survive and Others Die* (2007) that can be adapted to help make a presentation "sticky":

- Keep it simple—"You must be ruthless in your efforts to simplify—not dumb down—your message to its absolute core."

- Introduce the unexpected—"You can get people's interest by violating their expectations. . . . But to sustain their interest you have to stimulate their curiosity."

- Make it concrete—"Use natural speech and give real examples with real things, not abstractions."

- See that it's credible—"[W]e reach for numbers and cold hard data to support our claims. . . . But what's important is the context and the meaning of those statistics."

- Appeal to the emotions—"When possible put your ideas in human terms; '90 grams of fat' may seem concrete to you, but for others it's an abstraction."

- Tell a story—"We teach, we learn, and we grow through stories. Why is it that when the majority of smart, talented people have the chance to present, we usually get streams of information rather than story from them?"

The ideas that Reynolds popularizes on his blog are based on suggestions he finds in professional books, the countless hours he spends watching and delivering presentations, and his unique approach to Zen philosophy as it applies to the concept of design. This may all seem a bit esoteric, but these are the same principles we talk about when we discuss what makes good writing. Don't we often say that good writing is clear and concise and has a strong voice? Don't we look for details and examples to establish credibility? Even though we often preach a certain organizational style, aren't we amazed and delighted when a student provides something unique and creative? Why should digital presentations be any different?

Another set of design principles related to effective slide shows, although presented under a title that may not be appropriate for the classroom, is Joshua Johnson's two-part "10 Tips for Designing Presentations That Don't Suck" (2010a, 2010b), published on his blog, *Design Shack*. With self-explanatory headings, and great examples (they're well worth a visit to his blog), he suggests the following:

- Don't use a built-in theme.
- Use quality photography.
- Solid colors rock.
- Typography speaks volumes.
- Watch your readability.
- Simple is better.
- Avoid the bullet-point plague.
- Create clear focal points.
- Create a captivating cover.
- Make 'em laugh.

To further his points, a web search for "PowerPoints that don't suck" will lead you to a number of other examples, as well as the geeky-funny Don McMillan's "Life After Death by PowerPoint" video on YouTube.

On a more serious note, in an article in which he builds on the work of Duarte, Tufte, Reynolds, and other visual designers, Fred Johnson (2012) argues

> *Because the design of [slide] sequences begins not with a question about what facts the audience needs to know but with a question about how to explain or teach something complex and worthwhile to the audience, the content of the slides is less likely to be information to be copied or memorized and more likely to emerge as an occasion for significant interaction and thinking. (134)*

Crafting an effective presentation relies as much or more on design elements as it does on the text. There are also numerous resources that can help students learn to speak clearly and confidently. That said, this chapter will focus mainly on crafting the documents and the presentations effectively.

One other note: I am including the production of e-books in this chapter on presentations. While a presenter obviously delivers most of the message orally and a book delivers its message textually, these lines continue to blur, especially with the introduction of the many book-making apps for the iOS and Android operating systems. In 2012, Apple released iBooks Author software, which, like many slideware applications, allows anyone to create and distribute interactive books that can include audio, video, and hyperlinks to outside resources. As more readers move from page to screen, authors will increasingly not only write text but also design the layout for their books during the writing process. Crafting effective presentations and e-books share similar principles, and both are included in this chapter.

Viewing a Professional Mentor Text

A number of good presentations are available online, especially at TED.com, and the benefit of watching them is that you see not only a slide show but also the speaker delivering it. As digital writers design, revise, and prepare to deliver their presentations, they *should* focus nearly as much on their speaking as on the slides. However, this is usually not the case, exemplified by our students plowing through lists of bullet points and fancy animations without giving much consideration to using the slide show as only one element in a thoughtful, perhaps even stunning presentation.

Our mentor text is a talk originally given in February 2006, by Hans Rosling, a professor of global health at Sweden's Karolinska Institute. In this video, "Stats That Reshape Your Worldview" (http://goo.gl/4pwHJ), Rosling uses a slide show and an interactive data visualization tool to convince his audience that the Third World is catching up to the West. His first slide sequence is a "pretest" on global health he gave his students (arrows on the screen illustrate his main ideas). Throughout, he employs humor and effective transitions. About three minutes into the twenty-minute talk, he switches to a program that visualizes data about the world's population, including stats on health and poverty. He returns to the slide sequence and uses animation effectively to make the statistics come to life. Watching any of Rosling's TED talks reveals that statistics can be an informative, perhaps even pleasurable subject. If he had simply stood passively and delivered this talk as a series of slides with bullet points, he would not have been nearly as effective—or entertaining!

Scan to view
Rosling's TED talk.

Along with TED.com, there are other sources for digital mentor texts. The TED-Ed website (http://ed.ted.com/about) allows users to take videos, including any video on YouTube, and create a "flipped" lesson from that video. A lesson around a TED video could focus on content as well as form. By watching some of the best presenters in the world, we and our students can learn how best to deliver our own ideas to others. Common Craft (www.commoncraft.com/) and RSAnimate (http://comment.rsablogs.org.uk/videos/) contain great examples of animated presentations. Pecha Kucha (www.pecha-kucha.org/) and Ignite! (http://igniteshow.com) presentations generally consist of about twenty slides delivered in a five- or six-minute presentation. (Slides do not necessarily have to be set to advance at an even pace; varying the pace allows the presenter to personalize his or her message.)

In all cases, a quick return to the MAPS heuristic is useful as our digital writers begin to craft their presentations. While the media of presentations often come in the form of slides with text and image, that does not need to be a limiting factor. Also, as noted by Reynolds, telling a story with a "sticky" message is the best way to connect with an audience. And, finally, formats like TED, the animations from Common Craft and RSA, or the twenty-slide/five-minute format of Ignite! or Pecha Kucha offer some interesting situational constraints for digital writers.

Considerations for Presentations as Mentor Texts

Countless presentations are poorly designed, filled with weakly written content, or both. The best presentations are those in which the slides add an interesting dimension to the spoken words, and the oral and visual elements are delivered in tandem. Steve Moline, in *I See What You Mean* (2011, 10), says, "There are times when it makes sense *not* to write information in sentences. Visual texts sometimes do the job better."

Presentations can be more than a series of template-based slides. In *Literacy and Justice Through Photography* (2011), Ewald, Hyde, and Lord talk about adopting a different set of lenses, an apt metaphor for writing, too:

> *Sociology is, itself, about seeing. Like photography, it is a way of seeing. A sociological lens reminds us to look once again at the ordinary, and beneath its surface. It urges us to connect the large and small scale, the local and the worldly, the bewildering and the mundane. A camera lens likewise helps us look more closely at our world. As we frame pictures and time our shots, we slow down our looking, giving subjects due attention, seeing them anew. We isolate our subjects, deciding how to strip away or give context. We decide how others will see our subjects with framing that adds mystery or enhances meaning. (8)*

What is the purpose of the a digital writer's presentation and, in turn, what is the purpose of any particular slide in that presentation? Does the organization of a slide contribute to the audience's understanding the immediate purpose as well as the goals of an overall presentation? Is it enhancing meaning

Slideware, for better and for worse, is the currency that drives business meetings, conferences, workshops, and, more recently, much of the virtual space available in webinar windows. Despite calls from critics of software like PowerPoint and Keynote and attempts to help users move beyond templates and create more aesthetically pleasing designs (Tufte 2006), the fact remains that many bored, er, board meetings and second-grade animal reports end up being a series of formulaic slides. Prezi's (http://www.prezi.com) new zooming presentation software is a welcome technological advance, if used with intention. This chapter explores other options as well.

Slides created for school purposes are generally prescribed by the teacher, with little room for creativity. I strongly encourage you to remove any language about a set number of slides, minimum or maximum words per slide, or any other required templates from your presentation assignments or rubrics. We want to offer our students guidance, but we do not want to confine them to a particular set of rules that can destroy creativity. Instead offer models and general constraints.

A good presentation is the result of a great deal of writing that never shows up on the slides but becomes part of the words spoken by the writer. Presentations need to be crafted carefully by the writer/presenter to generate the maximum effect on the audience. It usually makes most sense for the person crafting the presentation to create alphabetic text at the same time as the slides, either as notes or a loose script. Above all, we need a better conceptual understanding of presentations. Tools like Prezi have an advantage over slideware, but there are other options, like creating a concept map and zooming in on the bubbles or repurposing slideware to make it more fluid. There are also options for creating screencasts or embedding links. Good presentations need not be limited to one speaker standing in front of an audience. Digital writers can be much more creative than that. Let's see how.

Curricular Connections

Presentations are often a unique blend of telling a story, sharing information, and making an argument, and the presentation gurus remind us that storytelling and "stickiness" are factors that go into delivering an effective presentation. It is not enough simply to share information or step logically through an argument. The presentation has to contain some sense of passion and purpose.

To return to the MAPS heuristic, the presentation tool is the media; the mode (genre) can vary. Different forms of presentation media allow us to do different things, and that affects the overall design, depending on the digital writer's audience, purpose, and situation. Summarizing a semester's worth of classwork is a much different task than describing the steps in a process, although PowerPoint, Prezi, or any other tool described in this chapter could be used effectively for both. Unlike Chapter 3 where I presented a table that outlines the various genre possibilities for different web-based texts, below I share some general thoughts about how presentations can be crafted in these different genres.

For Narrative Writing

While most often thought of as a means for delivering information or making a persuasive case, presentation software can also lend itself to storytelling. As already noted, Reynolds and other authors who focus on business communication and presentations believe that an audience's engagement is enhanced through storytelling. Helping students understand how to use slides effectively to share their stories, even if they are only smaller parts of informational or argument pieces, is crucial. For instance, could they use a screen image to enhance their mention of a particular moment or person in their lives? Might they insert a slide with an all-black or all-white background and one word or short phrase in bold print and contrasting color to make an emphatic point? The stories that we tell during our presentations can have powerful effects on how our listeners perceive what it is we have to say.

For Informational Writing

Probably the most common use for slide shows is to present information. But the ways we present information are not bound to particular templates or limited to bulleted lists. One or two words on the screen can be as effective as a bulleted list, and a simple chart or graph can convey what a much more complex set of numbers cannot. Nor do we need to limit ourselves to slides: students could create an infographic (information graphic) and zoom in on different areas while presenting it. Helping students understand how to effectively create an appropriate introduction, the right kinds of supporting evidence and examples, and a satisfying conclusion—all connected with a consistent design, color scheme, and choice of fonts—is central to the craft of digital writing.

For Argumentative Writing

One of the key tenets in argument writing is that the writer must present both sides of the debate, not merely persuade with overwhelming evidence from one side. Slide presentations provide interesting opportunities for students to present counterarguments. What if counterarguments were presented in colors that contrast with those used for the arguments in favor? What if the student included video footage of another student presenting counterarguments, then responded to those arguments orally in real time? Unlike in a traditional academic paper, these types of turn taking and transitioning from one idea to the next can be made visually and orally. For some great examples of how to enter the academic conversation and phrases you could teach students to use to express contrasting viewpoints, I recommend *They Say, I Say: The Moves That Matter in Academic Writing* (2011), by Graff, Birkenstein, and Durst. Or point students to a list of transition words like the one found on the Purdue Online Writing Lab's website: http://owl.english.purdue.edu/owl/resource/574/02/.

TECH CONNECTION: THINKING OUTSIDE THE BOX WITH OTHER TOOLS AND TECHNIQUES FOR CRAFTING PRESENTATIONS

There are other options for creating slide show presentations or resources to include in slide shows, possibilities that help students craft presentations in critical and creative ways. Some of these tools, like Glogster and Capzles, get a fuller treatment as examples later in this chapter. Others I'll simply mention below. When using any kind of animation or automatic sequencing tools, the presenter should think carefully about the overall message being delivered as well as the design of the particular slides. Duarte (2008) notes

> *Every change, no matter how subtle, creates distraction. Every animation, no matter how well intended, affects an audience's ability to grasp insights. And that's not to say animations are a bad thing; they should be used only to help an audience process information. But for some reason, many presenters struggle with selecting animation wisely.*
>
> *As a presenter, you might quickly recognize the opportunity to design content effectively. But you also need to think about designing—intentionally—the time-based elements within a presentation. Animation is not last-minute icing on the cake; it's a key communication strategy. (180)*

As you prepare any type of digital presentation, sometimes the fonts, images, backgrounds, and other layout features you wish to use are either too complicated or simply not available. Here's a quick trick: you can design a slide in either Power-Point or Keynote and then convert it to a TIFF or JPEG image you can import into any document or web-based tool that accepts images. That way if you feel you really need a slide-like look for part of a presentation, you can import these images.

Table 4.1	Alternatives to Stand-Alone Slide Presentations
Online Share Shows	▪ www.slideshare.net (upload PPT or Keynote, then share in Google Hangout)
Recorded Presentations	▪ www.authorstream.com (turn your slide show into a video) ▪ http://present.me *and* http://vcasmo.com (video-record yourself talking next to your slides)
Video/ Multimedia	▪ http://voicethread.com ▪ http://littlebirdtales.com ▪ www.pixorial.com
Posters	▪ http://edu.glogster.com
Interactive Timelines	▪ www.capzles.com
Word Clouds	▪ www.wordle.net ▪ www.tagxedo.com
Infographics	▪ http://visual.ly ▪ www.easel.ly ▪ http://infogr.am
Sketching/ Whiteboards	▪ www.educreations.com (iPad) ▪ https://cacoo.com (works in Google Hangouts) ▪ www.scriblink.com ▪ http://cosketch.com ▪ www.scribblar.com ▪ http://flockdraw.com
Screencasting and Screencap- ture	▪ www.techsmith.com/jing.html ▪ www.screencast-o-matic.com ▪ www.screenr.com ▪ http://evernote.com/skitch/

Exploring the Digital Writing Process for Presentations

The design principles of Robin Williams and the notes about "stickiness" from Garr Reynolds apply here as well, and Nancy Duarte (2008) offers the following set of additional axioms:

> *Effective slide design hinges on mastery of three things: arrangement, visual elements, and movement.*
> - *Arrangement—contrast, hierarchy, unity, space, proximity, and flow*
> - *Visual Elements—background color, text, and images*
> - *Movement—timing, pace, distance, direction, and eye flow*
>
> *(88)*

Duarte goes on to discuss ways we can create movement between slides based on the transitions we use and where images are placed. For instance, a rectangular box on the right edge of one slide could then lead to the next slide being "pushed" across the screen, revealing the point of an arrow connected to that rectangle.

The design of any individual slide does not stand in isolation from the rest of the slide show, just as the writing of any paragraph is not separate from an entire story or essay. However, this does not mean that we should fall back on templates when considering how best to organize our slides. An overview of an effective presentation composing process is shown in Table 4.2.

Prewriting and Drafting Presentations

Although the tendency of any digital writer creating any digital text is to begin by opening a new file in whatever program he or she intends to use, the best place to start is with pencil and paper. Nowhere is this more important than in designing a presentation. Set aside all the rules of thumb you've been told about designing slides—no more than six bullet points, never use animation in a serious business presentation—and visualize what it is you hope to say to your audience. Think in pictures, even sketch some if that's useful. The goal is to break free from the templates, think of the central visual metaphor, perhaps even the color scheme, and focus on the main idea.

Table 4.2	An Overview of the Composing Process for Presentations
Prewriting and Drafting	■ Start with a blank sheet of paper or perhaps a few boxes outlining the slides or frames you intend to use. ■ Skip the template, and create your own: focus on colors and fonts. ■ Imagine the animations and transitions: will there be animations or other media effects? If so, for what purpose?
Revising and Editing	■ Remind yourself of the "stickiness" factors: simple, unexpected, concrete, credible, emotional, storylike. ■ Edit for visual appeal, not just grammatical correctness.
Publishing and Assessing	■ Along with your slide show, develop a complementary handout (not just a printout of the slides). ■ Assess the form and function; give feedback on the design and delivery as well as the content of the presentation.

When your students are ready to begin crafting their presentation in the software or web-based app of their choice, encourage them to skip the templates and create their own. (While some younger students may benefit from having a pre-designed template to help them organize their thoughts, by middle school, and certainly by high school, students could be designing their own.) Depending on the assignment, they could design a logo for the presentation or tweak the fonts used. At some point, though, spending too much time on the design takes away from the overall effect of delivering the message. Strike a healthy balance. As a preservice teacher once shared with me, the time spent doing these types of digital writing tasks can make us lose sight of the forest and see only the trees (in short, she said that designing slides is "not really writing"). It is our task as teachers to help our digital writers see why and how designing slides is, indeed, a task about crafting that concerns them.

Finally, imagine the animations and transitions. Will there be animations or other media effects? If so, for what purpose? In what ways do these effects help you transition between ideas, either linking them together or contrasting them with one another? Just as a writer uses these rhetorical elements to craft an effective essay or story, the digital writer preparing a presentation must think consciously about when and how to use media judiciously for rhetorical purposes.

TECH TIP: PLACES TO FIND GOOD IMAGES

Assuming that they are using it in a transformative manner, students have the fair-use right to any copyrighted image they find on the Internet (Hobbs 2010). Still, encouraging them to go beyond the search engines and investigate specific sites that specialize in images can be useful. In particular, because the creators of these sites often add tags or comments, students have the benefit of an added human element. Of course, the images they find may still need to be tweaked by an editing program such as the free online tool, Pixlr (http://pixlr.com). Nevertheless, in lieu of creating their own photographic compositions, students can find free images at the following sites (the first four gleaned from Reynolds [2008], the last a collection of links from award-winning librarian and edublogger Joyce Valenza):

- www.morguefile.com
- www.imageafter.com
- www.sxc.hu
- www.everystockphoto.com
- http://copyrightfriendly.wikispaces.com

Revising and Editing Presentations

As students prepare to deliver their presentations, remind them of the "stickiness" factors: simple, unexpected, concrete, credible, emotional, and storylike. Have them count how many of these factors, rather than counting slides, images, and words, are evident in their and their peers' presentations. This kind of qualitative response instead of a quantitative list will help students get the gist of what it means to craft an effective presentation. Along with thinking about and drafting their speech, they should edit the presentations for visual appeal, not just grammatical correctness. Finally, as a way to rehearse or even prepare their presentation for a wider audience on the Internet, invite students to use one of the presentation recording tools or screencasting programs mentioned earlier.

Publishing Presentations

Garr Reynolds, in *Presentation Zen* (2008, 67), notes the three parts of a presentation: "Slides the audience will see; notes only you will see; handout to be taken away." I first encountered the idea of creating a complementary handout (rather than a printout of slides with blank spaces in which to take notes) from visual design guru Edward Tufte (2006), and I often create a one-page handout (perhaps using the back side as well as the front) for my audiences. Sometimes I include a few key slides with additional notes, but the handout is primarily additional text and graphics and a listening guide. In recent years I've been projecting a QR code on the screen and inviting people to navigate directly to my website to find a handout. Nevertheless, despite all the new technology and the ability to publish slide shows online, a physical handout can still be useful, and I'm strongly considering a move back to the one-page paper handout. A one-page handout gives the audience all the information they need.

Figure 4.1 shows a screenshot of a handout I created for a presentation at the 2011 NCTE annual convention. My colleague, Kristen Hawley Turner, and I condensed the main ideas from our presentation into one 8.5″ by 11″ sheet of paper. What do you notice about the way the handout is created? How does it adhere to Robin Williams' CRAP principles of good design? What might you change to make it more effective? How do you think it connected to our presentation?

Assessing Presentations

We need to consider not only the number of slides but also the quality of the content. We need to move beyond templates and assess the form and function. More important, we need to give feedback on the design and delivery of the presentation. Following are applicable Common Core Speaking and Listening Anchor Standards 4, 5, and 6 (http://www.corestandards.org/ELA-Literacy/CCRA/SL):

Presentation of Knowledge and Ideas

4. Present information, findings, and supporting evidence such that listeners can follow the line of reasoning, and the organization, development, and style are appropriate to task, purpose, and audience.

5. Make strategic use of digital media and visual displays of data to express information and enhance understanding of presentations.

Figure 4.1

Sample Handout to Complement a Slide Show Presentation

Writing Our Inquiry   NCTE 2011: G.52 - 9:30 am to 10:45 am 11/19/2011

"That's not writing": Examining Novice Teachers' Perceptions of Digital Writing

Kristen Hawley Turner   Fordham University   krturner@fordham.edu
Troy Hicks   Central Michigan University   troy.hicks@cmich.edu

In this forthcoming article, we highlight the experiences of Kristen and the Teach for America (TFA) corps members who she taught in a course about the teaching of writing during spring 2011. Kristen invited Troy to act as an outside consultant for the students as she introduced these novice English teachers to digital and multigenre approaches as viable alternatives to traditional essays. Though we had first hoped to document how to integrate digital writing into English teacher education, based on our work with Kristen's students, the inquiry quickly turned to a deeper exploration of why teachers of writing must embrace multimodal composition.

Below, we invite you to hear the voices of pre-service teachers, including their perspectives on the process and products of multimodal writing as well as the tensions they felt both as multimodal writers themselves and teachers of writing. Quotes were taken from reflective papers and a transcribed Skype conversation; italics added by the researchers.

Perspectives on multimodal writing

Multimodal writing as textual transformation	Multimodal writing without textual writing	Multimodal writing as a limiting/limited form of writing
"I really changed my idea of how students are able to communicate via writing while I was doing a multimodal assignment for this class. It ended up being a video of images and being posted on Youtube, but it began by me sitting down and *drafting what I wanted to say* in the video. I *edited and revised this script* like I would any other piece of writing, but my product was drastically different from a typical written assignment and I think that my message was much *more effectively communicated through this other mode/genre*."	"This piece allowed me to see what *kind of thought, planning, revision, and creativity* goes into creating a piece without writing. It also allowed me to *communicate a preserved message* with an audience without traditional writing. This revealed to me that writing is no longer the only way to preserve one's ideas for an audience or for one's own reflection. Writing is now accompanied by *other means of composition.* "	"I found my own experience with digital writing this semester to be *very frustrating*, and I often found my ideas and arguments to be *diluted and a little stifled* by my use of technology, and it comes from my own biases against technology.... I found it very difficult to make the arguments as I would be able to in my writing in any sort of digital mode. I'm wondering now at the end of the semester is *how I would use technology in my classroom with writing* taking my own experiences into account."

Tensions as writers and teachers of writing

Multimodal writing is not "writing"	Conflicting views of the self	External pressures define classroom practice
"I would still say I have stubborn, maybe conservative, clinging to semantics. *I don't like applying the word 'writing' to things like making videos or like podcasts and stuff.* Although I value those greatly... for some reason I would prefer to term it something different."	"I have this stark contrast of myself as a writer and myself as a teacher of writing. They're really different to me. As a writer, I see all these *liberal possibilities* of what writing means, and yet when I get in front of my 6th graders it turns into a *very formulaic, how do they do it [persona].* "	"One of the big reasons that I feel like I really shouldn't do that [digital writing] is because I was *never asked* to do it in college, and I feel like a lot of the things we are doing here I really enjoy but I think that *nothing else has caught up to that* and so... that's *kind of foolish* of me to take that time... to do something *that isn't frivolous but isn't necessary either.*"

6. Adapt speech to a variety of contexts and communicative tasks, demonstrating command of formal English when indicated or appropriate.

Verbs used everywhere in the standards—*emphasize*, *integrate*, *clarify*, *strengthen*, *add*—provide excellent guidance for creating specific criteria for evaluating presentations. Students need to be aware of how the "stickiness" factors and design principles connect with what it is we expect them to do. Presentations, including both spoken and visual elements, should:

- Emphasize salient points by focusing on key ideas through choices in font and color, limited amounts of text, and the inclusion of a visual metaphor.

- Integrate appropriate (with regard to both content and length) multimedia and visual displays as a coherent part of a broader presentation. These visual displays, when possible, should be created by the student, although limited examples of existing materials found on the Internet can be used with appropriate citation.

- Clarify information by using appropriate multimedia effects such as panning, zooming, and highlighting, or otherwise animating limited selections.

- Strengthen claims by providing a variety of evidence that meets the criteria of given contexts. For instance, in a report on illegal immigration, appropriate evidence may include charts showing the overall immigrant population, a short video clip of an immigrant talking about how she has crossed the border illegally, and a snapshot of language from a recent congressional bill about immigration.

- Add interest by periodically using transitions, a black screen, or slides with an alternative background or image in conjunction with verbal cues that signal the audience to pay attention.

If we articulate these standards clearly and encourage students to connect the spoken and visual elements, they will be better able to identify the traits of effective presenters and more apt to include such elements in their own slide shows.

I am often asked about the best place to find rubrics for multimedia work. As I mentioned in *The Digital Writing Workshop*, Bernajean Porter's Digitales site (http://digitales.us/evaluating-projects/scoring-guides) has what I think are very useful evaluation guides for multimedia. They are interactive and allow you to choose particular criteria to use in your own rubric. In addition, a brief and useful resource created by the composition faculty at Indiana University, "Crib Sheet: Assessing Multimedia Projects," can be found at http://digitalis.nwp.org/resource/ 1135. Both emphasize the cumulative effect of employing media in strategic ways; just because digital writers can add multimedia elements, especially in presentations, it does not necessarily mean that they must do so. Judicious use of images, videos, music or other effects can have a positive influence on an audience, whereas overuse simply turns people off.

Examples of Student-Composed Presentations

Erin Klein invited her students at Madison Middle School, in Adrian, Michigan, to create multimodal presentations about the historic voyage of the *Titanic*. While some students created slide shows and others created videos, two alternative formats chosen by students are particularly interesting.

In this poster created on Glogster (http://goo.gl/mFseN) Hunter Brewer combines a number of historical images of the *Titanic* and its passengers with written text that complements and explains the images. The poster (see Figure 4.2) displays a variety of visuals related to the *Titanic*: five images of the ship, four of artifacts, two of interior areas, and one of the crew, as well as an embedded video. The background includes bursts of fireworks, and unfortunately some of these images obscure portions of the text. Some of the text sounds very encyclopedic, perhaps taken from another source, but the text underneath the image of the staircase is framed as answers to questions: "What was on the *Titanic* to eat?" "What kind of drinks do they have?" It could have been useful if Hunter had elaborated on this approach, making each image a link to interesting representative facts. Still, Glogster is a versatile space in which students can meld different media, especially text and images, including videos.

Scan to view Titanic poster.

Thinking again about MAPS, craft questions related to this poster include:

Online Poster for Titanic Project

Figure 4.2

- How are the poster's conceptual categories and visuals used to support those categories organized?

- As a presentation, a poster offers no "introduction" or "conclusion," although readers generally scan it from the top left, in a Z formation to the bottom right. What are the major stops along that Z pattern for a viewers' eyes? Words? Images? Headings?

- Glogs allow for hyperlinks. How might Hunter employ hyperlinks effectively to provide his reader with more information?

As a second example, in his Capzles timeline (http://goo.gl/Z97Cl), John Ambrose puts a series of images in sequential order, interspersed with four short documents. See Figure 4.3. While Capzles also allows users to put specific dates on images and group them in albums, this particular example is laid out linearly. John has charted the history of the ship from its initial construction to the launch to hitting the iceberg to its rediscovery decades later. Each segment of the timeline ends with a one-paragraph document summarizing what happened to the ship during that period.

Again, some MAPS-like craft questions related to this timeline include:

- What other textual features could be included to help guide the reader?

- How should the variety of pictures—historical images as well as modern renderings—be acknowledged or cited?

- Is the insertion of a text document between the sections helpful or distracting? How might John have crafted a different kind of transition between the sections?

Both the poster and the timeline move beyond the boundaries of slide shows to create something interactive and aesthetically pleasing. While having the topic set by the teacher limited the kinds of images students could use, they were still able to present their ideas in different formats—the poster images clustered by topic and the timeline focusing on chronology. Encouraging students to present their ideas in formats that move beyond simple templates is one way we can help them become better digital writers, and tools like these, when employed thoughtfully, can help us reach that goal.

Scan to view
Titanic timeline.

Again, in this piece of student work and in others in this chapter, we have replaced images that the student used with a description of the images. While it is considered fair use for students to use copyrighted images for educational purposes, it is not fair use to print them in a book that is being offered for sale. For more information about fair use and copyright law, see page 9 of the introduction.

Figure 4.3

Partial Online Timeline for Titanic Project

The Titanic

[photos of the construction of *Titanic*]

DOC

[photos of the interior of *Titanic*]

High School: Presentations

In his "risk taking, mistake making" classroom, Andrew Schoenborn, a teacher at Mount Pleasant High School, in Michigan, expects his students to think critically and creatively. He invites them to create a variety of digital writing pieces, from blog posts as the Frankenstein monster to "This I Believe" digital video essays. One of the projects he has his high school seniors produce is a literary analysis that goes far beyond writing an essay. Working collaboratively, students must apply an interpretative lens to one of the texts they have read in class and create a dynamic, multimedia presentation on Prezi. For this example (http://goo.gl/3c8xq), a group of students started with an inquiry question—"How does Lady Macbeth defy gender role conventions of her time?"—and developed a conceptual map of their thinking, sequencing ideas within the presentation.

To see the students move between ideas in the Prezi and presenters speaking, go to this book's companion wiki page, and click on the video recording of these students leading their presentation (it's a little over twenty-one minutes long), so I have noted the times for the three transitions in the annotations in Table 4.3.

Scan to view
Macbeth Prezi.

Table 4.3	Images from the "Macbeth and Gender Roles" Presentation

The students use the first segment of the Prezi to state their question: "How does Lady Macbeth defy gender role conventions of her time?" For this presentation, the frames advance vertically; the line at the bottom of the circle leads directly to the second frame, shown below.

MAPS Question: In designing this opening sequence, as well as the overall look of their Prezi, what choices have the students made about how to construct their argument?

From the initial frame, the Prezi advances to the next frame (0:10), zoomed out in this screenshot, which has a central circle with three lines arcing out to satellite circles. Within the main circle, which defines "gender roles," is a smaller circle describing a typical woman's role in 1605. Each of the three smaller circles shares an example of how Lady Macbeth defies a gender role, and each has a YouTube video embedded next to it.

MAPS Question: How does the layout of these examples demonstrate the group's approach to categorizing their importance? Is this effective?

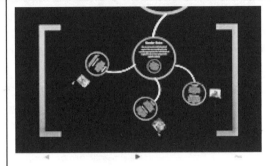

The videos, created by the students, show an image that represents Lady Macbeth or another character in the scene; music plays in the background, with the lyrics displayed, karaoke style, over the image. On the Prezi website, you can only hear the song and see the lyrics. In the wiki-page video of the students' presentation, however, they talk about the specific plot elements and actions of Lady Macbeth. This happens at 1:46, 5:30, and 10:00.

MAPS Question: Does this additional visual/audio text work well for you as a viewer? What might the students have done to craft a more comprehensible text?

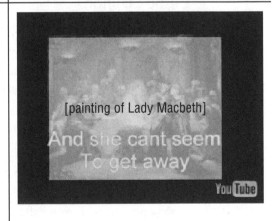

Table 4.3	Images from the "Macbeth and Gender Roles" Presentation (*cont.*)

After these extended examples, the students move into a deeper analysis, asking directly, "So how did Lady Macbeth defy these conventions?" This circle links to three smaller circles, interspersed with four images.

MAPS Question: How does the design of this frame, including the images and border, affect our viewing? How do the students organize their argument?

Zooming in, we are able to see how the students define Lady Macbeth's defiance of gender roles, then contrast it with an image of what she "should" have been like as well as a quote from the play.

MAPS Question: How does it help our comprehension to see that the students will present three related ideas? Would a traditional slide show provide the same overall effect?

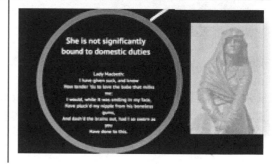

E-Book Options

As I mentioned earlier, it may appear strange to see an option for publishing digital books in a chapter on presentations. Writing and speaking are similar, but distinct enough, language arts skills that this connection may seem not to make sense. In some ways, I agree; I would never want students to get so lost in creating a presentation—or an e-book—that they lose sight of the story they want to tell.

However, I include e-book production for three reasons. First, students are going to be consuming more and more books digitally. While printed books will not be totally usurped, students are going to be interacting with e-books, and having some sense of how to design them will be important. Second, many of the new e-book platforms allow for the integration of multimedia: students can design digital writing projects composed of multiple components. Finally, as discussed in the chapter on craft, a number of teachers and researchers have been paying much more attention to visual literacy and its effects on argumentative, informational, and narrative writing. Earlier, I noted Katie Wood Ray's book, *In Pictures and In Words: Teaching the Qualities of Good Writing Through Illustration Study* (2010), as one smart example of how we can help students use drawing not only as a thinking tool but also to enhance the ways in which they craft their stories. Steve Moline's *I See What You Mean: Visual Literacy K–8* (2011) focuses on more informational types of visuals. E-books take this a step further. Students can draw an image on paper and convert it to a digital image, create images using computer software, or integrate other types of communicative visuals such as charts, photos, or tables. Clearly, integrating visual literacy and alphabetic literacy is important, and creating e-books allows students to combine these two skills.

The example in Figure 4.4 is from Amber Kowatch's second-grade classroom at Franklin Elementary School, in Ludington, Michigan. Every student in Amber's classroom used an iPad during the 2011–12 school year, and results of this project will be shared in the upcoming documentary. *Look I'm Learning: A Story of Digital Learning Success* (www.lookimlearning.org). Amber's students created a variety of informational e-books about the animals they were researching, with some of the books including multiple-choice quizzes or short videos. They also created digital picture books. *Summer* by Callie Chaney is a strong example of a digital picture book, even though it lacks any interactive features. I think it gets to the heart of what Katie Wood Ray is arguing for in her book: students can use images and words together to tell a powerful story.

Scan to view
Callie's e-book.

Let's look at how student writer Callie accomplishes that goal. I recommend that instead of analyzing the book page by page and identifying every craft move, you read through the entire text once focusing on the words, a second time focusing on the pictures, and a third time looking at the words and pictures in tandem. A few MAPS questions to guide your reading:

- How does Callie use repetition of words and specific images/colors to achieve a particular effect in this story?

- How does Callie invite you, as a reader and viewer, into the story with particular words and images?

- How does the use of an ellipsis on the first page of the text contribute to the overall sense of how the rest of the text is structured? How is this structure supported by the images that follow?

Figure **4.4**

Images from the Summer E-Book

Summer

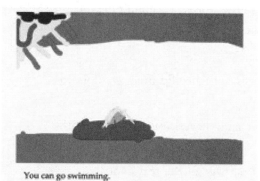

Page 1

I like summer best because...

Page 2

I love the sweet smell of flowers.

Page 3

You can plant a garden.

Page 4

You can go swimming.

Page 5

You can see fireworks.

Page 6

Figure 4.4

Images from the Summer E-Book (*cont.*)

You can have a cookout.

Page 7

You can even get ice-cream.

Page 8

I like summer because you can do so many fun things!

Page 9

- Finally, how does the use of the superlative (*even*) on the penultimate page, as well as the picture on that page, contribute to a sense of closure?

One other note about crafting a digital text, especially one that relies on both verbal and visual repetition, is that you can have students design a background and use it as a template, adding items appropriate for the various pictures. For instance, pages 2, 3, and 5 of Callie's e-book use essentially the same sky-and-grass background. Callie could have reused the identical background for each, superimposing the images of the flowers, herself holding the flower, and the grill, respectively, managing her time and digital resources more effectively.

Conclusion

Presentations have come a long way in the past few years as more and more web-based and mobile apps hit the market. Given the ubiquity of presentations in all aspects of our work lives, not to mention our participation in civic organizations and other opportunities for public speaking, students are going to need a variety of skills both as digital writers and as speakers. Broadening the range of tools at their disposal is essential if we want them to become critical and creative, crafting "sticky" presentations that can be viewed in a variety of flexible ways. Moreover, students have to learn how to collaborate with others across time and space to generate interesting, sometimes interactive presentations.

What is compelling about presentations as a digital writing tool is that so many other forms of media and composition can come into play. From typography and photography to graphic design and data visualizations, the possibilities for breaking away from templates and creating new ideas are endless. Students can also create—and embed—audio and video media into their presentations, topics we take up in the next two chapters.

CRAFTING AUDIO TEXTS | 5

I think good radio often uses the techniques of fiction: characters, scenes, a big urgent emotional question. And as in the best fiction, tone counts for a lot.

—*Ira Glass*

Since the dawn of human history, we have been composing stories and sharing them through an oral tradition. While some may disagree with Socrates' assertion that writing would destroy our memory, we can all agree that there is still power in the spoken word. In the earliest part of the twentieth century, radio brought a variety of programming to the world, including the legendary broadcast of *War of the Worlds*; spoken words, sound effects, and music combined in some magical way still continue to captivate our imagination. Even recorded books are big business nowadays, with "celebrity editions" of popular titles. Also, podcasts—both from amateur and professional sources—have become a part of our news, education, and entertainment diet.

As a longtime listener of National Public Radio (NPR), I have become accustomed to the high quality of their multifaceted audio productions. From news stories that involve the voices of a reporter, experts, and in many cases a "person on the street" to more elaborate shows such as *This American Life*, *Radio Lab*, and *On the Media* that incorporate music and sound effects, each NPR segment carries a distinct tone. In contrast, the commercial radio stations I sometimes listen to offer a very different kind of aural assault, with loud commercials, opinionated and vocal hosts, and repetitive sound bites. Regardless of your political stripe, NPR appeals to a variety of listeners and offers many great models for audio mentor texts.

Informational reporting is only one of a variety of text types we hear on NPR. From conversational narratives presented on *Story Corps* to argumentative debates on *Intelligence Squared*, we have many models to share with students. One way to use these mentor texts is to adapt Kelly Gallagher's article-of-the-week strategy, in which he has his students write responses to and summaries of a compelling non-fiction text (Gallagher 2012). By sharing an audiocast (with the accompanying transcription, provided for most programs on the NPR website), and analyzing it with an ear toward understanding current events, we can use news stories as digital mentor texts.

As a next step, thinking about these stories as digital texts, we can invite students to analyze the craft of audio production. MAPS-like questions to ask include:

- How is the piece introduced? What details are given in the overview?

- Does the reporter/narrator start talking immediately? Is there a musical segue? Background sound?

- Who is invited to talk? Experts? Persons on the street? People with similar or conflicting views on the topic?

- What "B roll" audio footage is included? For instance, do ambient noises occur in the setting for the interview, or was it recorded in a sound booth?

- How does the reporter introduce new ideas or transition to contrasting ones?

- Who speaks last? What are the voices, sounds, or music at the close of the piece and how does that leave you with a final impression?

"Pulling Back the Curtain," a segment of the NPR show *On the Media*, is an interesting piece on how producers create the "NPR sound." John Solomon reports that NPR hosts, producers, and to some extent even the guests know that most interviews are not broadcast live and will go through some postproduction. Solomon wonders

> *By making everyone sound better and increasing the amount of content in the broadcasts, it would seem to be a win-win-win for the network, its sources and, most importantly, its listeners.*

*Yet is there a small sin of omission? NPR may not be actively mis-
leading listeners, but we all know that they don't know how we create the
cleaner and more articulate reality. (Solomon 2007, emphasis added)*

That the conversations we hear on NPR are not always "real" could be seen as a negative feature. Yet all news outlets have to edit their stories for time constraints and other journalistic necessities. The point is that our students, as listeners—and as digital writers—should be aware of the way these audio texts are crafted.

Numerous genres can be featured in audio texts, but some are more suited to it than others. What if Nicole's dialogue between her teeth in her multigenre research project (Chapter 3) were recorded as a podcast? How might she (and perhaps a few of her classmates) have created a different voice for each tooth? What sound effects could have invoked a fearful visit to the dentist's office? Would music (or Muzak) have added to the overall tone?

While audio texts generally get short shrift in our curriculum and instruction, the speaking and listening standards of the CCSS offer a variety of opportunities for introducing them in connection with the language arts skills we must address. Students might write formal scripts or less formal outlines of talking points that need to be elaborated with details and examples. These skills require deep, sustained listening. Given that we live in a sound-bite culture, our students must listen attentively to spoken texts, both live and recorded, in order to become effective digital writers prepared for future study, work, and civic engagement.

Listening to a Professional Mentor Text

A recent NPR story on uses of social media by teens and young adults (Sydell 2011) has many craft elements that make it an effective audio composition. To listen to a podcast, scan this QR code or go to (http://goo.gl/FQ90A). As you listen, note the moves the reporter and producers make to craft an effective audio text:

Scan to listen to
the podcast.

- *Intro*: As a signal to the listener, one of the musical transitions for the show *Morning Edition* plays for the first three seconds.

- *Host*: One of *Morning Edition*'s hosts, Renee Montagne, introduces the context for the story for about twenty seconds.

- *Reporter*: Laura Sydell opens by stating, "If you sit down with some teenagers and ask them if people are mean on Facebook, heads nod."

- *Example from a person on the street*: The audio switches to Sydell's interview with three teenagers recorded in a high school cafeteria. They comment about friendly and not-so-friendly encounters on Facebook.

- *Expert*: About two minutes into the story, Sydell introduces an expert, Amanda Lenhart, from the Pew Research Center's Internet and American Life Project. She cites and provides information from a report.

- *Close*: Sydell returns to introduce one more comment from one of the teens, and the piece closes with a different clip of "outro" music.

Returning to the MAPS considerations again—mode, media, audience, purpose, and situation—to what extent does Sydell, and her producers, accomplish the goals of an effective audio text? What media elements mattered most? What audiences might this piece appeal to and why?

Considerations for Audio Texts

Readers can browse written texts and viewers can fast-forward through videos to get a sense of their content, but there's no real way for a listener to preview an audiocast unless there's a transcript, and even that will not convey the full sense of what the producer intends. Tone, ambient noise, music, and transitions matter just as much as the words that are spoken. Listeners are placing their trust in the producer of the audio text, hoping it will be worth listening to, so an engaging initial impression is imperative. Much like an effective lead in a written piece, the beginning of an audio text must capture the listener's attention and give some sense of what's to come.

Also, audio texts may be the one form of digital writing most reliant on the *voice* of the writer—both the writing trait of "voice," as well as the writer's tone when reading his or her words aloud. Even though most English teachers probably never thought that they would be voice coaches, a few tips from the pros are helpful to share and practice with our students. For instance, Toastmasters International (2011) recommends tips for breathing and relaxation, as well as for articulation and projection. Varying your pitch and volume, slowing your speed, and pronouncing words properly all help, too.

Finally, audio texts—especially the digital kind described here—lend themselves to including sound effects and music. There are many options for creating music and recording sound effects in programs such as Apple's GarageBand and the open source audio editor Audacity (http://audacity.sourceforge.net). If time or material constraints prevent creating these features from scratch, students can take advantage of many other resources, including the following:

- Creative Commons Licensed Sound Effects (http://freesound.org)

- Creative Commons Licensed Sound Music (www.jamendo.com/en)

- Public Domain Sound Effects (http://commons.wikimedia.org/wiki/Category:Sound)

Curricular Connections

Students' speaking and listening can be enhanced by having them create digital audio texts. A quick scan of NPR programs and Apple's podcast directory reveals a number of shows, both specific titles and broad genres, that can be used as models of different text types. Some shows blur genres; the stories on *This American Life*, for example, often inform the audience or make an argument for or against a specific idea as much as they tell a compelling narrative. Still, the list in Table 5.1 will help you and your students locate examples to use as mentors. NPR, Stitcher, and TED have mobile apps that allow users to stream or download podcasts to listen to while on the go; Apple has its own Podcast App. (The term *podcast* has come to encompass both audio and video productions, as evidenced by the "video podcasts" or "vodcasts" available. However, *podcast*, in this chapter, refers to audio recordings.)

Table 5.1	Audio Text Types

Narrative	Informational	Argumentative
Short segments such as *Story Corps* on NPR	Main news programs such as *All Things Considered* and *Morning Edition* (NPR)	*Intelligence Squared* (NPR)
Longer segments such as *This American Life* on NPR	Conversational NPR news programs such as *Fresh Air*	TED Talks (http://ted.com)
The Moth Radio Hour (NPR)	Topical NPR programs such as *On the Media* and *Radio Lab*	Political NPR talk shows such as *The Diane Rehm Show* and *Talk of the Nation*, which feature people on both sides of the issue
www.LearnOutLoud.com ("free audio and video" link)	*Grammar Girl* (and others in the *Quick and Dirty Tips* podcast series)	National Forensics League TV (http://nfltv.org); although recorded debates are not available for free, the topics are thoroughly introduced in short videos that can be used as models for podcasts
Audio Book of the Month	Podcasts of *New York Times* and NPR book reviews	
Poem of the Day podcasts by the Poetry Foundation		

Examples of Student-Composed Audio Texts

From my own research and conversations with colleagues, it appears that podcasting has not made its way into nearly as many classrooms as other forms of digital writing. Still, the power of the human voice and the flexibility of crafting audio texts—from impromptu conversations to highly scripted and rehearsed performances—indicate that we need to explore audio texts in our digital writing workshops. Tim Saunders, the science teacher who I mentioned in Chapter 3, has students include podcasts of their conversations in their science journaling wikis. Robert Rivera-Amezola, featured in *Because Digital Writing Matters* (National Writing Project, DeVoss, Eidman-Aadahl, and Hicks 2010), has produced a podcast resource on the Digital Is website (http://digitalis.nwp.org/resource/2701). The clips of his enthusiastic fourth graders reading their scripted reports for a service-learning project are priceless. Even the mainstream media have picked up on the power of podcasting as a digital writing tool (see Williams 2012).

This example of a group of middle school students' digital book trailer for *Artemis Fowl: The Lost Colony* (Colfer 2009) (http://goo.gl/HIAvZ) was provided by Lindsay Stoetzel, a colleague from Gull Lake, Michigan. The students participated in literature circles for many class periods before they created the script. Following a model developed by Rozema (2007), Lindsay invited them to "decide how to talk about their texts—as outsiders to the story, as the characters themselves, or as both" (35). They then spent a few days in the computer lab searching for clips of sounds and music to add to the mood of their podcast and used Aviary's Myna Audio Editor to craft a multivoiced production, complete with sound effects and a musical score. (Unfortunately, Aviary took the Myna Audio Editor offline in September 2012, yet this type of editing can still be done with Audacity, Garageband, or other programs.)

Scan to listen to book trailer.

For the recording, the students created three separate tracks for three different voices: two narrators speaking both within and about the story as well as a boy's voice as one of the characters. A total of six tracks stretch across two minutes and thirty seconds. As shown in the screenshot in Figure 5.1, Aviary's multitrack editor allows the user to see both the tracks themselves as well as the amplitude of the sound waves in each track. This display makes it easier for students to insert audio at just the right point, noting where one track ends and another begins or where it could overlap. I invite you to listen to the podcast first, then continue reading.

At the beginning of the recording, the music loop in track 1 kicks in and crescendos while the narrator says, "The time spell is breaking. No one is safe." The two short sentences catch the listener's attention. Then a crash is heard, and the narrator begins the story: "Number One was torn. . . ." This is an excellent introduction, a pattern common in many movie trailers that translates well to a digital book trailer. Narration continues, and then the sound of a laser that happens about fifty-five seconds into the recording can be seen in track five.

At about 1:15, the narration and then the music stop. A new background loop begins, and the narrator changes perspective, talking *about* the book, not as if he were a character in the book: "The novel *Artemis Fowl: The Lost Colony*, by Eoin Colfer, is a book of mystery and adventure with a twist of insanity." The summary alternates between the two narrators until about 2:15, at which point one narrator states excitedly, "*Artemis Fowl: The Lost Colony* is now available at the GLMS library!" followed by the imperative, "Read it! Read it! Read it!" Taking a nod from commercial radio, the narrator then says, in a fast-paced voice, much like one we'd

Figure 5.1

Screenshot of the Aviary Project File for the Book Trailer for
Artemis Fowl: The Lost Colony

hear in a pharmaceutical ad, "*Artemis Fowl: The Lost Colony* is not the first book of the series," and "We're not responsible for any people who do not like this book."

Listening to this audio text, we know that these middle school students have enjoyed and thoroughly understood the book they have read. They clearly know the genre of the "trailer"—a persuasive text that encourages others to read the book while including details and examples that give a glimpse into the narrative. They also employ the audio medium metacognitively: adjusting the pitch of their voice, as well as the pacing, they emulate typical tones and phrasing heard in other radio commercials. In short, their podcast emulates the genre quite well.

Looking at the audio editor screenshot, however, reveals that the students did not have the very brief introduction in mind from the get-go. The narrator saying, "The time spell is breaking. No one is safe," appears as track 6, not track 2. Lindsay's students had carefully scripted the recording so that the three of them would have an opportunity to read different segments, including those in which they imitated the characters' voices (tracks 2, 3, and 4). After they finished the initial recording, including various loops and the later sound effects, they went back and recorded a brief introduction that hooks listeners, making them want to find out more.

To conclude our consideration of this example, consider the following MAPS questions related to how students crafted this piece:

- What effect does each piece of music have on the overall tone of the podcast?

- To what extent do the characters' voices support the purpose of the podcast? Are they too distracting at times?

- In their attempts to add humor at the end, do the writers of this podcast meet the expectations of their audience? The assignment?

TECH CONNECTION: TOOLS FOR CRAFTING AUDIO TEXT

For many years, the free, open source audio editor Audacity has been the tool of choice for relatively simple recording tasks that nevertheless require multiple tracks. While Audacity is still available for PC, Mac, and Linux—and Apple offers its own GarageBand software as a standard program with its new computers—the options for recording and saving items online has recently expanded. For recordings that are essentially all talk, websites and apps such as AudioBoo (http://audioboo.fm), Chirbit (www.chirbit.com), or SoundCloud (www.soundcloud.com) allow users to record their voice and save it online. While you could include music or sound effects in the background, they would have to be part of the original live performance. These tools are therefore best for simply recording voices. The best audio editor for student use is still Audacity. Students have the ability to view multiple tracks, fade sound in and out easily, cut and paste audio tracks as they would text in a word processor, and export the audiocast as an MP3 file.

In my work with preservice teachers, I continue to use the "This I Believe" essay as a model for crafting audio texts. Dawn Reed and I have described the process of helping her students craft these audio essays (Reed and Hicks 2009), and she was gracious enough to share her unit plan in *The Digital Writing Workshop* (Hicks 2009). The "This I Believe" essay helps students understand the recursive nature of the writing process, moving beyond the retelling of a personal experience and working with ideas in a thematic or metaphorical way. While these texts generally do not include other audio elements such as music or sound effects, the experience of recording (and, often, re-recording) one's voice is an experience my students value. In trying to develop your stance as a writer, there are few better ways than listening to your own voice as a reader.

Exploring the Digital Writing Process for Audio Texts

An audio text can be created quickly as an in-class activity with little editing (Sewell and Denton 2011) or as a sustained project over time (Chase and Laufenberg 2011; Rozema 2007; Smythe and Neufeld 2010). As I emphasize throughout this book, the essential element is that students craft digital texts with intention. It is one thing to grab a smart phone, click record, and post a quick conversation online using a podcasting service such as AudioBoo; that's appropriate and acceptable for some tasks. It is quite another to ask another person for an interview, preview your topic, ask questions that will lead to thoughtful comments, and edit the resulting recording into a coherent story with appropriate music and sound effects.

Table 5.2 is not a set of hard-and-fast "rules" for the types of audio texts our students can craft with mobile phones, tablets, and computers, but it does give a sense of what can be done given various contexts, equipment, and amounts of time. The focus is on *content creation* and *production value*, terms related to how digital writers find or develop content and then craft that content through postproduction. The description in Table 5.3 outlines a complex approach, one that would occur over many days.

Prewriting and Drafting Audio Text

When we compose an audio text, we face particular opportunities, challenges, and technical decisions, as well as decisions about craft. Even though the final recording may be presented with a written script (or transcript if created as a conversation), we cannot fully appreciate the text unless we listen to it. In my own teaching, in the

Table 5.2	Decisions About Content Creation and Production Value for Audio Texts	
	Lower Production Value	**Higher Production Value**
Higher Degree of Content Creation	Recording a scripted conversation/text between several voices; may require minor editing before posting online	Recording a multivoiced text, including original music, sound effects, and ambient ("B roll") sounds; requires major editing
Lower Degree of Content Creation	Recording an impromptu conversation or interview and posting it online with no additional editing	Recording a rehearsed conversation and adding music or sound effects found online; requires minimal editing

Table 5.3	An Overview of the Composing Process for Audio Texts
Prewriting and Drafting	■ Scripting text and reading as compared to doing an interview ■ Recording additional sounds or "B roll" footage as compared to download-ing preexisting recordings ■ Recording volume levels and evening out the sound
Revising and Editing	■ Recording tracks for each voice ■ Adding echoes, pitch modulations, or other effects ■ Aligning music and sound effects with voice tracks
Publishing and Assessing	■ Creating a final audio track in a compatible format such as MP3 ■ Uploading to a class website or web service for audio files ■ Differentiating between the quality of the content and the form of the product

workshops I conduct, and in the conversations I have with in-service colleagues, I stress the distinct difference between a print (and even a video) text and an audio text. Audio texts are difficult to preview and review without, knowing the part that you want to fix. Often times, I suggest that students record only a portion of an entire script, such as a few sentences or a paragraph, and do so for each section. Then, they can shift those smaller portions of text along the timeline as they see fit.

When students are crafting an audio text, we need to be particularly attentive to how we invite them to speak for themselves and how they invite the voices of others. There are numerous examples of a small segment of a quote used out of context (especially by politicians). Many times in a news report, an eyewitness or expert is cut off midsentence or midthought because the report has been edited for time. How students present their questions and respond to the answers, verbally and nonverbally, during interviews and recording sessions can prompt either comfortable, full thoughts or constrained responses.

Depending on the type of text being crafted, a digital writer will also want to think carefully about ambient noises in the interview/recording environment and the types of sound effects or music that might be added in postproduction. If a student is crafting a narrative about a hike in the woods, capturing ambient noises may be difficult, if not impossible, depending on whether the recording is being done in the woods, as well as the sensitivity of the recording equipment. It might be easier to pull in sound effects during postproduction rather than create original "B roll" audio. Or the clatter and noise of a restaurant setting may obscure the conversation. In that case, the student may first record the background footage, then record the dialogue between characters in a quieter setting.

When editing audio text, technical considerations also need to be kept in mind. It's important to modulate the volume of individual tracks; voices may need to be prominent at some points, music or sound effects at others. Ideally, all the recording should be done in one sitting with the same equipment. Nothing is as disruptive to a listener as hearing the narrator speak in rich, full tones in one segment, then hearing that same voice sound thin and scratchy in another. This could be an intended effect—if the narrator or character has changed locations, say—but it is generally just distracting. So, even when recording segments, as suggested above, students need to be sure not to change any of the settings from one to the next.

Students may record their work in one take, but it rarely comes out perfect the first time. There are two ways to solve this problem. One, the student can leave the mic running even if he messes up. Pausing to take a deep breath and then starting over isn't a problem; he can go back later, cut the final track into segments, remove the glitches. The second option—at risk of sounding repetitive—is to record individual segments, a few sentences or paragraphs at a time. This method helps the student avoid the trap of reading slower or faster from frustration or impatience, and the smaller chunks are easier to edit during postproduction. However, if the student changes computers or microphones or even adjusts the settings from one segment to another, the sound of his voice may be drastically different.

Lindsay Stoetzel allows students a full day in the computer lab to become used to the audio recording program and listen to different music selections. Although some could consider this practice a waste of time, she argues for it.

> *We then begin by spending a full day choosing and saving music. . . . This could seem like a lot of time to waste in class, but students use this time to brainstorm the structure and approach for the piece, develop a clear mood, and sketch out what scenes may be included and require certain types of music. I also always do this first because it is a lot of fun and gets the students hooked and excited to get to the writing part. (Personal communication, July 23, 2012)*

Before the students enter the computer lab to search for music samples, Lindsay has them listen to examples of podcasts and think about how the music and sound effects enhance or detract from the overall message. Students are listening to and choosing music with intention, developing craft in the process.

Revising and Editing Audio Texts

During this phase, students can easily get caught up in the bells and whistles. Adding and deleting sound effects, searching for just the right song, or rerecording their voices can eat up an inordinate amount of time. It is usually best to have students record any narration, scripted or unscripted, and then download those files into the Audacity editing program for arranging and editing. Any files that need to be re-recorded can be deleted and replacement files downloaded. Again, Lindsay offers some advice.

> *For the script, there is a rubric we review, including areas such as the integration of meaningful quotes from the book and credit for contribution to the Google Doc, as well as typical writing elements (hook, conventions). I judge the written element separate from the final podcast production. I also require rough drafts to be reviewed and revised before students can move on to recording. We talk about how to keep the reader's attention and discuss areas of confusion where more info is*

needed. That tends to be the hardest element—communicating an idea without the use of visual cues. So the division of the script and setup of parts is crucial to whether or not the final product will be understandable. (Personal communication, July 23, 2012)

Lindsay designs the podcasting assignment so that students must include several voices. One of the distinct advantages of recording these segments separately is that students can play with the order of the segments or, if appropriate, have voices overlap. Helping students make wise decisions about how and why to raise or lower their voice or modulate its pitch, include an echo effect, introduce music, or insert an effective pause is part of the revising and editing stage.

Audio texts often begin with a distinct introduction that tells listeners what they are about to hear. Think of an anchor introducing a segment in a newscast, or the beginning of an audio book where the speaker announces the title, author, and publication information. While digital writers can post audio texts online or release them as podcasts without any formal introduction, even a brief one can help orient the listener.

One of the most powerful features of audio texts is the possibility of including a number of voices. Dawn Reed, whose podcasting curriculum for a "This I Believe" unit was featured in *The Digital Writing Workshop*, suggests that having students craft a common introduction for their essays is a great collaborative digital writing process in and of itself, as well as an opportunity for students to discuss their beliefs. She has each student make a clip of his or her initial "I believe" statement, and then the students, as a class, order the clips, paying attention to each speaker's tone and the overall effect. They end up with a sixty-second or less introduction that everyone adds to her or his individual audio recording. Even if a student has only one other line of dialogue recorded by a friend or family member, that additional voice is highly effective. Other voices encourage students to think about different perspectives and help them understand the ways that unique voices contribute to a project.

Publishing Audio Texts

Two technical elements to consider in the distribution phase are how to format the audio text and where to store it. While cross-platform compatibility continues to improve, saving audio files in a widely accepted format makes the most sense. This generally means MP3 so it can be played by any computer or compatible audio device. Then the file needs to be uploaded to a blog, wiki, or service listed above. Students could create individual accounts, but then the files have to be found and accessed individually. The other option is to set up a single account for the class, share the login information, and have students post to that common account. Consider how you plan to listen to these files. Will you sit at your computer or do you want to have access to them on the go, such as from a mobile device? Where and how we ask students to share their files matters a great deal, especially if we want to distribute them to wider audiences. Some pointers are provided in Table 5.4.

Assessing Audio Texts

Lindsay Stoetzel introduces an informal assessment tool by inviting her students to vote on their podcasts—best use of multiple voices, best use of music, best overall, and similar categories. She grades script content and overall podcast quality (to include multiple voices, sound effects, music, and other digital writing features) separately. As evaluators of student work, many of us skim an entire piece before evaluating it in depth and go back to look at particular paragraphs or video frames in order to make specific comments. How do we best accomplish this while listening to a recording? The MAPS heuristic is useful here, especially since the intimacy of an audio recording can sway our opinions about students' work. What are the goals that we have for students using audio media as compared to making an emotional impact on their audience? For instance, stuttering or unnaturally long pauses in a student's speech would not be evident in a traditional alphabetic text; in an audio text these features would be immediately apparent and quite possibly have a negative influence on our opinion.

Also, depending on the duration and purpose of the audio text, creativity in the recording process could be a component of the final assessment. For a journalistic piece, you might set criteria for how many people must be interviewed, as well as how many facts or other sources to include. These are both technical and rhetorical decisions. Technically, students would have to identify opportunities to conduct several interviews in settings without too much background noise, and may perhaps even have to record "B roll" footage to supplement the interviews. Rhetorically, they might cite a person on the street as well as an expert, and also turn to other websites, books, or media sources.

Table 5.4	How to Save an Audio Text to a Website and a Web-Based Service

Uploading to a Class Website	Uploading to a Service
1. Once the audio file is saved, log in to your class website (on Wikispaces in this example). 2. On the page where you want the audio file to appear, click the edit button and place your cursor at the point of insertion. 3. Click the file button and then choose to upload the audio file. Once the file is inserted into the page, click save.  4. The audio file will now appear as a playable link directly on the page.  **Advantage:** Audio files are saved directly to your class website and even to students' individual pages. **Disadvantage:** It is impossible to subscribe to these individual files as a podcast feed and listen to them consecutively.	1. Once the audio file is saved, log in to a web-based audio service (AudioBoo in this example; on AudioBoo files must be less than three minutes long). 2. Upload the file, provide a name, and continue.  3. Once the file has been processed, it will allow you to go to the homepage of the file. On that page are links to subscribe to the podcast via iTunes or RSS.  4. Should you choose, you may embed the audio file in a webpage, as well as have it available as a podcasting feed. **Advantage:** Audio files are saved directly to Audio Boo without clogging your class website's space. As a teacher, you could create one generic account and have students save to the same account so that all the podcasts are available in a single feed. **Disadvantage:** The files must be shorter than three minutes, unless you upgrade to a Pro account.

One of the main challenges in assessing audio texts is the time it takes to listen to them. Of course, with our own smartphones and mobile devices, we can get lots of listening done while in transit, so perhaps that is one advantage of having students submit audio projects. As you guide your students through the process of writing and recording, the formative assessment you offer along the way will help them craft a well-timed, thorough, perhaps even witty script. When listening to the final product, then, you should be able to enjoy what the students have created as an overall piece. The audio text should be able to stand on its own.

In the end, assessing audio texts becomes a balance of process and product, content and form. From the very first seconds of the recording all the way through to the last, students must make well-informed, creative, critical decisions about how best to maintain the audience's attention while not going overboard on any particular element, especially music or sound effects. They need to have distinguished the qualities of a prepared speech from those of a spontaneous bit of talking.

Conclusion

As I mentioned, I do not see podcasting employed as often as other forms of digital writing such as creating presentations, websites, or videos. Still, I do meet teachers, especially foreign language teachers, who have students record themselves and listen back to their pronunciations and overall tone. A podcast is also a useful way for students to reflect on their performance.

I hope that we as language arts teachers continue to support our students' learning in this oral form. As globalization continues and English (for better or worse) becomes the dominant language for business and education, we must help students understand that the power of their spoken words is incredibly strong. Inviting students to record and then listen to their own voice can also open up conversations about dialect, multilingualism, and the denotations and connotations of particular words and phrases. While we certainly want our students to be strong readers and writers, the fact remains that in today's digital world they will be using their speaking and listening skills as much, if not more. Whether students are constructing an argument, organizing information, or developing a narrative, possessing the digital writing skills to be able to create audio text can only help them be more intentional in their extemporaneous speech. Next, we imagine what they can do by crafting digital videos.

CRAFTING VIDEO TEXTS | 6

I think it is very important that films make people look at what they've forgotten.

—*Spike Lee*

From the earlier writings of Marshall McLuhan (1964, 2005) and Neil Postman (1985, 2005), right up to media literacy scholars of today such as Renee Hobbs (2011) and Richard Beach (2006), those of us teaching the English language arts have been interested in how media, especially video, affect our lives. Today, many forms of media surround us and, in various ways, invite us to read, listen, view, click, as well as—with the advent of smart phones and tablets—tap and touch. Critics and educators interested in creating media-savvy students have long argued that we need a cautious, even skeptical approach to the types of media we consume. Asking questions such as "who created these media and for what purpose?" helps guide us to be critical consumers of the world shown in television shows, films, music videos, and commercials and, today, by people with their own webcams and mobile phones. New technologies allow all of us to explore what otherwise might be forgotten.

Video texts—of live events with real people; of scripted, well-produced television shows or films; of hand-drawn, computer, or stop-motion animation; and many other forms—may be *the* form of digital writing many of us need to learn to convey information in the twenty-first century. While alphabetic texts, in both print and web-based forms, are still a crucial component of our literacy practices, the degree of our video consumption points to a world in which moving images speak louder than words. From professionally produced movies and television shows to footage you and I capture with our mobile phones, literally thousands of hours of video texts are created, uploaded, and viewed every minute of the day.

How do we invite our students to become both smart consumers of video texts and, as digital writers, smart producers of them as well? As we think about using visual literacy to craft digital video texts, we have the opportunity to guide our students toward systematic and imaginative uses of video in our digital writing workshops. While all writing involves a process that is recursive and often messy, composing digital video has the potential to be even more so. Penny Kittle (2010) describes her students moving recursively from writing in their notebook to composing a digital video: "We write in notebooks at the start of class the next day: take one part of your movie and craft that scene into words, I say. Use all of your skills as a writer to make that image live on the page" (50). Back and forth, the writing process unfolds on paper and on screen.

Your goal, like that of all good writing teachers, is to guide your students through the composing process, helping them make smart decisions about everything, from whether to make a live-action video or a screencast all the way through the final stages of adding narration and transitions, then preparing to publish. Just as there are many types of videos, there are many types of composing processes. This chapter is a general outline of how to examine a video as a mentor text and how to guide students through the digital writing process to create their own video texts. One caveat before moving ahead. I understand the substantial amount of time needed to compose thoughtful and thorough digital videos, and I can also understand why we might see this falling outside the purview of the English classroom, lending itself to a class on film making instead. Still, I strongly encourage you to teach toward the recursive nature of writing, on page and on screen, as you work with students on these types of compositions.

Viewing a Professional Mentor Text

Finding a digital mentor text to view and critique is no longer the challenge it used to be. While some schools still have strict filtering policies, most teachers with whom I've worked have the ability to access a video from YouTube or other video-sharing site and play it for their class. When teaching visual literacy meant reserving a TV cart and wheeling it into your classroom or cuing up a DVD to the right scene, I could understand teachers' reluctance to teach visual media literacy. Today, however, when we can stream everything from recently released movies to last night's sports replays, and there are thousands of high-quality (and many more thousands of not-so-high-quality) digital videos to choose from.

A video with wide-range appeal for students in grades 4–12 is the short, stunning "Evolution" (http://youtu.be/iYhCn0jf46U). Dove's Campaign for Real Beauty, in the 2000s, featured this seventy-five-second video, which provides many points of entry for a conversation about media literacy and how videos are crafted. In this time-lapsed photo shoot, a woman's image undergoes a dramatic transformation through make-up and hairstyling and finally is edited with a computer. I find three things about the craft of this video particularly interesting and worth talking about with your digital writers, again in light of the ideas raised by the MAPS heuristic that focuses on mode, media, audience, purpose, and situation:

Scan to view
Evolution video.

- *Time-lapse photography*—Time-lapse photography has long been a staple of nature films and other types of videos showing a process. My children love watching *How It's Made* and the plethora of nature and cityscape films in which motion too subtle to be caught by the human eye becomes very pronounced. In the "Evolution" video, a woman goes from "normal" to "supermodel" in a little over sixty seconds, exposing the hypocrisy of beauty product advertisements and, in turn, the negative effects on women's self-images.

- *Screencasting*—When the film shifts from the model and the photo shoot to the computer's graphic design program, it moves from live-action film to what amounts to a screencast, where motions on a computer screen are captured in real time (but sped up for the video). The end of the video goes back to live-action shots to expose the true nature of how the image was constructed. What if students took screencasts as they construct their own projects and used them to reflect on the process?

- *Image construction*—This commercial shows the process of constructing an image, whereas normally we ask students to deconstruct existing images and videos. How might students create digital writing about constructing or critiquing an advertisement?

While Unilever, Dove's parent company, was criticized because many of its other brands continued to produce misleading or sexist advertisements, the Campaign for Real Beauty revealed how a big advertiser was willing to pull back the curtain and help average viewers become aware of the marketing machine.

As we struggle to help our daughters (and sons, for that matter) understand the cultural constructs of beauty, this text is worthy of our attention. We can use it as an example of the integration of live action and a computer screencast; the brevity and directness of a message; an idea conveyed visually with no additional narration; or an advertisement that critiques or parodies existing advertisements. Whatever your purpose and whatever tools your students will use to create their own video text, focus on the idea of a concise message that critiques an existing cultural norm. Whatever the topic being explored or the age of the writers working on the task, the lessons learned from "Evolution" are powerful.

Considerations for Digital Video Texts as Mentor Texts

Video texts present many interesting options; we want to choose carefully what we show our students as a model for them to emulate. Students can (and will) go to YouTube and watch a variety of digital mentor texts (some that we, as adults and teachers, may be loathe to describe as such). But if we want our students to be critical consumers and producers of text, we need to understand that anything they watch, purposefully or incidentally, can be a mentor text—traditionally scripted acting, real-time events, claymation or other stop-motion photography, satires and parodies, film trailers, music videos. Bill Bass, an educational technology integration coach from St. Louis, Missouri, suggests the following three lenses through which we can teach our students to view videos as digital mentor texts:

- As examples of *content* that we can remix or use as a model for creating our own (for instance: a reenactment, a news clip, or a lip-dub video) (Bass 2012a)

- As examples of *technique* for setting up and framing shots (Bass 2012b)
- As examples of a *process* for documenting how something is created (an art project, a dance routine, a computer application) (Bass 2012c)

These categories of mentor texts help us understand that videos can serve many purposes and that just as we teach students to "read like a writer," we need to help them "view like a videographer." While we do need to read, view, and critique the media, we now have increasingly easier opportunities to create media as well. Students in a digital writing workshop can create compositions that include text, image, video, and voice. These compositions can range from a short, personal introduction recorded with a webcam to a podcast recording of a personal essay to a documentary film. And all of it can be shared online.

There is definite craft involved in creating the various types of videos. The setting, lighting, costuming, acting, and camera angles all play a role in live-action productions; the timing and sequence of images, narration, sound effects, and music come into the play when designing basic videos. Either way, digital writers have to make decisions about how their words, spoken and written, connect to and enhance what's happening on screen. Choices about timing, background music, transitions, and other effects have to be balanced with the overall goals for the video text. No matter what media are employed, in the service of what genre, our students have to make choices about how and why to use media elements to compose compelling narrative, informational, or argumentative texts. The digital writing process allows them both to create their own media documents and to better understand the types and purposes of the media they see each day.

Curricular Connections

Even though we may feel that the Common Core State Standards limit our language arts focus to reading and writing, we *can* think about them in relation to composing digital video texts. Take anchor standard 8 for writing, for example: "Gather relevant information from multiple print and digital sources, assess the credibility and accuracy of each source, and integrate the information while avoiding plagiarism." These principles are very much in line with what National Council of Teachers of English (NCTE) and International Reading Association (IRA) have been calling for in broader language arts standards over many decades. Composing a live-action video of themselves speaking extemporaneously or delivering scripted narration can help students meet many of these standards. With careful attention to the craft of digital writing, we can help our students meet not only the speaking and listening standards but many of the writing standards as well.

The CCSS suggest that students be able to compose in the three broad text types—argumentative, informational, and narrative—all three of which can be represented in digital videos. Moreover, the CCSS require students to "use technology, including the Internet, to produce and publish writing as well as to interact and collaborate with others." Digital videos can be shared on the Internet. Some video productions use only still images in sequence; others are a mix of still and motion photography. In some, students narrate or impersonate characters; others use music or sound effects, and still others combine all these elements. While recording oral histories or conducting interviews, students become active researchers; other types of video rely more on secondary research (gathering existing images and repurposing them). Table 6.1 outlines a number of possibilities for creating video texts in a digital writing workshop. Later in the chapter, we examine four video projects created by elementary, middle, and high school writers. Using their own digital images or original artwork (as well as images collected from the Internet) combined with

Table 6.1	Types of Video Texts

Possibilities for Video in Narrative Genres	Possibilities for Video in Informational Genres	Possibilities for Video in Argumentative Genres
▪ Personal memoir ▪ Retelling a story from the perspective of an existing character/person ▪ Creating an original story in a genre such as historical fiction, science fiction, fairy tale, myth, or legend	▪ Minidocumentaries ▪ Feature news stories ▪ Oral histories ▪ Reenactments ▪ How-to demonstrations ▪ Book, film, music, or art reviews	▪ Exposé-style minidocumentaries meant to articulate a certain position ▪ Public service announcements ▪ Political advertisements ▪ Debates

narration, music, and/or sound effects, students can craft digital videos that feature narrative, information, or argument.

Even with all these possibilities, the most difficult part of crafting a video/ multimedia text—as with crafting a print-based text—is knowing not only what to put in but what to leave out. Bernajean Porter, author of *DigiTales: The Art of Telling Digital Stories* (2005), suggests that we use media elements judiciously, asking whether we are merely *decorating* our story, *illustrating* a concept, or *illuminating* our viewers through the combination of media elements. Digital writers should ask themselves whether the media they are choosing are being used simply because they can be or whether there is a rhetorical purpose for that use. You can put in transitions, sound effects, and captions, for instance, but are these the best media elements to help tell your story? Are you making good decisions as a digital writer?

Many resources offer more thorough and thoughtful discussions of video making than I can offer here: three are Nikos Theodosakis' *The Director in the Classroom: How Filmmaking Inspires Learning* (2001) and John Golden's pair of books *Reading in the Dark: Using Film as a Tool in the English Classroom* (2001) and *Reading in the Reel World: Teaching Documentaries and Other Nonfiction Texts* (2006). Golden's books in particular include deeply detailed definitions of film terminology and cinematic effects, as well as a useful glossary. Again, I understand that the line between teaching digital writing in the context of an English class and jumping straight into a filmmaking class may be a thin one, and I encourage you to think about the most effective ways to integrate such a project into your particular context. What we will do here is learn from gifted teachers who are using video in their classrooms and take what they are understanding about visual literacy and apply it to digital writing.

As students consider some of the possibilities afforded by digital editing, the creative possibilities for revision grow, too. In his classic *After THE END* (1992), Barry Lane taught us how writers can play with time by exploding moments and shrinking centuries. Now, with digital video, we can shift time in new ways, slowing images down and speeding them up and moving instantly across time and space. The various visual and audio effects serve in much the same way as word choice, sentence structure, or punctuation do in print texts: each has a different rhetorical purpose and effect.

Considerations when editing digital video include:

■ *Narration*—Does the video require narration? If so, who is speaking and what is the point of view?

■ *Panning and zooming*—How might a digital writer use these built-in effects for adding motion to photographs to invite us to focus in on one detail or broaden our view?

■ *Repetition*—How might a digital writer use the same image, sound, or transition to accentuate a particular point?

■ *Time effects* (fast-forward, rewind, slow motion)—How might a digital writer think about slowing down and speeding up time?

■ *Film effects* (sepia, black-and-white, and so on)—How could these filters be applied to flashbacks, flash-forwards, or alternate takes for dramatic effect?

■ *Transitions* (scene to scene)—How might fading to black, simulating a page turn, sliding across the screen, or using a jump cut contribute to the video's pacing and sequence?

■ *Sound effects and music*—How might a digital writer use sound effects or music to accent something from the text, signal a transition, or provide background noise?

■ *Captions and text*—How can a digital writer use text—environmental text within the image/video, as well as captions, titles, thought balloons, and other textual features—to accentuate the story?

The MAPS heuristic helps writers decide how and why to compose their texts in certain ways, and this general approach can be useful for getting started. As we consider how to help students craft video texts, a few broad questions to keep in mind follow:

■ What is the mode (genre) of the video and what are the benefits and constraints of other media (text, image, audio) in relation to that mode? How might you invite students to make different choices if they are going to craft a digital story (personal narrative), a documentary (informational), or a public service announcement (argumentative)?

■ In what ways does the goal for this video invite students to choose video-editing software?

- Are they interviewing participants or setting up events to be acted out?

- Will they be photographing their own images or finding them on the web?

- Does this particular assignment favor some media over others (for instance, still image with voice-over versus live-action shots)?

■ To what degree will the video feature students' own images, videos, and voices? Outside media they gather and use under fair-use provisions of the copyright law or Creative Commons licensing? How will they blend these various media elements to create a composition that is uniquely theirs?

■ What are your overall goals for the assignment? Is the focus on speaking and listening or on constructing an argumentative, informational, or narrative text? How much time will students have for the task, both in and outside school?

These broad questions guide us toward questions about craft, the most important questions we can ask our digital writers. Crafting digital video is a multifaceted process, one that blends rhetorical choices of the genre with technical elements of video production.

TECH CONNECTION: TOOLS FOR CRAFTING VIDEO TEXTS

Students now have numerous tools available to them as creators of digital video texts. Standard on almost any recently manufactured computer are movie-making tools such as iMovie (Mac) or Windows Live Movie Maker (PC). While I have not found an online video editor that includes all the features of iMovie and similar programs, WeVideo (www.wevideo.com) comes very close, and there are a variety of web-based video creation tools. Alan Levine lists many of them in "50+ Web 2.0 Ways to Tell a Story" (http://50ways.wikispaces.com), although the specific features and abilities of some programs may not give you the flexibility you would like. For instance, Animoto (http://animoto.com) allows you to upload images and automatically make interesting blends from one to the next, but you don't have much control over the timing (at least with the free version). One other particularly useful tool for young digital writers is Little Bird Tales (http://littlebirdtales.com), which has a simplified and visually appealing interface.

The benefits of using web-based tools rather than a program on a specific computer are many: students can access their work at home, school, or anywhere with an Internet connection; media files are stored remotely and cannot be lost; many web-based programs allow collaborators to view and revise; and students are able to publish their work, often with a choice between a private link or a public document. Although using web-based video-editing tools does not solve access issues inherent to the digital divide outside school, this solution is much better than having access to a program only on one computer at school. No matter what video tools you and your students use, the main focus when creating a digital video should be the craft of writing and helping writers make smart craft decisions.

Exploring the Digital Writing Process for Video Texts

As I've already stated, we, as writing teachers, need to focus on the writer, then the writing, and finally on the technology. Sometimes this means beginning a technology-rich project away from the computer. It is possible to begin any multimedia project with a sketch, a storyboard, even a conversation. Just as talking and drawing are important ways writers begin their writing process, these steps are also important in a digital writing process. Within the recursive pattern of moving from the written word (the script and production ideas) back and forth to the video, writers should focus on the main idea of telling a story, making an argument, or providing information. The features of any particular program are simply a means to help them accomplish that goal. Table 6.2 is an overview of that process; more detail on each step is provided in the following sections.

Prewriting and Drafting Video Texts

Students create multimedia compositions in essentially three ways: by designing all their own media; by repurposing existing media; or, most often, by composing a text that uses their own media as well as those created by others.

When creating their own media, students have a variety of options. Of course, they can use tools such as digital cameras, digital video recorders, digital voice

Table 6.2	Overview of the Composing Process for Digital Video Texts
Prewriting and Drafting	■ Scripting and storyboarding ■ Choosing an appropriate program (e.g., iMovie, Photostory) or website (e.g., WeVideo or Little Bird Tales) for production ■ Gathering and creating images, graphs, or other visuals by using an image search or creating images on the computer ■ Gathering and creating additional media: music, sound effects, "B roll" background

Revising and Editing	■ Importing and adjusting media
	  ● Importing media into a movie-making program or website
	  ● Adjusting timing and transitions between images
	  ● Adding opening and final credits, possibly including the documentation of sources in the video (if appropriate to the genre)
	■ Narrating and timing
	  ● Recording one's own voice
	  ● Creating multiple videoclips
	  ● Adding multiple voices

Publishing and Assessing	■ Sharing video in an accessible video format, preferably using a service such as YouTube or Vimeo ■ Inviting responses by framing questions for viewers in the description or comments box (formative assessment) ■ Balancing your assessment of the work in relation to process and product, especially related to the overall goals for the genre (summative assessment)

recorders, and, increasingly, mobile phones to capture images, audio, and video. To write text, they can use mobile devices, tablets, word processors (perhaps with a digital pen instead of a keyboard), or pencil and paper (the text can then be scanned into a word processor). In the process of creating any and all of these media documents, students need to attend to a variety of ideas related to composition. With an audio recording, sound quality is essential: the microphone must be placed properly, the setting for the recording must be quiet (or feature quiet ambient noise if that is important), and speech must be clear and articulate. With videography and photography, the lighting must be appropriate, the camera angle should be skillfully chosen, and a variety of shots need to be taken so there will be editing choices. While it can be difficult for students to create good media to use in their projects, the process helps them understand the intellectual work that goes into creating such materials.

Still, there are times when it is both more desirable and, to be honest, more efficient to use existing media. Perhaps you want your students to create a video that critiques an existing commercial; it would make little sense for them to do so without referring to the original video. When repurposing existing media, students must begin with some basic understanding of how to search for and find different types of media online. Whether they are searching for photos, videos, sound clips, music, fonts, or other effects, they must be conscious of where they are getting these materials as well as how they cite their sources. Copyrighted materials can be employed under fair use, but students need to make sure the use is transformative. This critical thinking process begins even before they type a term into the search bar and continues through the moment they publish their work online. With these things in mind, students can move forward in the process of scripting, revising, and publishing their digital video projects, to include storyboarding, gathering and creating images, and editing.

Scripting and Storyboarding

A challenge in any writing situation is simply getting started. With a project that involves creating images as well as writing words, it can be even harder. Overwhelmed by so many technical choices—transitions, music, and other media elements—students can quickly lose sight of the central goal: to compose a clear, coherent text. Many books and articles describe the process of digital storytelling in detail (Kajder 2004 and Porter 2005, for example). The point that I want to make here is that our writers need to imagine their ideas both visually and in writing.

The ReadWriteThink website includes a storyboarding chart (www
.readwritethink.org/files/resources/printouts/Director.pdf) on which students can
plot the characters and action, the setting, the camera position, and any sound effects or background music. While this is not the typical comic-book-style storyboard provided as a bonus feature on some DVDs, it helps students articulate the
movement of the story. As students move into composing their digital video, the
storyboards and initial ideas can guide but shouldn't restrain them. (Some teachers
skip a formal storyboard and jump right into the movie-making program, but it
helps to have students step away from the computer screen at some point and think
conceptually about what they are trying to accomplish as writers.)

Skills related to collecting and organizing multimedia elements must be taught
explicitly along the way. If students are assembling media, not creating their own,
they can use social bookmarking or shared online spaces to keep track of the elements they identify. In particular, I have found Dropbox to be a useful tool for
gathering media and accessing it across devices: see the Tech Tip below.

TECH TIP: USING DROPBOX TO SAVE AND ORGANIZE MEDIA ELEMENTS

Dropbox is an online storage tool that allows you to
upload and synchronize
files (including images,
audio clips, and docu-
ments). Dropbox maintains
a copy of these files in a se-
cure location you can access
using any device with an In-
ternet connection; you don't have to transfer files from device to device. This way,
students can have access to all of their media files—images, videos, audio, music—
in one spot, which can also be set up as a virtual drive on a computer. Also, creating
subfolders for the different kinds of media—images in a folder, sounds in another—helps digital writers stay organized. A detailed, step-by-step screencast for
setting up an account with Dropbox and installing the tool in your web browser is
available at www.dropbox.com.

Creating and Gathering Images, Graphs, or Other Visuals

(See also the complementary section in Chapter 5, which focuses on gathering and creating sound effects, music, and narration.)

As the guru of visual design, Edward Tufte, has said, "The minimum we should hope for with any display technology is that it should do no harm" (Nadel 2003). Any images used in a digital video—whether photographs, drawings, or graphs—should enhance the video's message, not detract from it. Gathering or creating and then organizing and arranging images is critical work in the process of crafting a digital video, and there are three primary ways of doing so.

- Using search engines and other online databases to find images and videos, whether copyrighted, licensed under Creative Commons, or in the public domain

- Creating your own images or videos

- Creating graphic or visual representations with software programs or data visualization tools

Searching for Images and Videos

Students can search for images using Google, Yahoo!, or Bing; bookmark them with tools like Diigo; and save copies locally or with a cloud-based storage tool such as Dropbox. (Depending on students' age and skill level, you might also ask them to record pertinent information such as the photographer's or artist's name and the date the image was created.) Again, Joyce Valenza has compiled a great resource with her wiki to find many images that are royalty free, either as licensed under Creative Commons or because they are in the public domain (http://copyrightfriendly.wikispaces.com). No matter where students get their images and videos, you will need to coach them to document their sources. Often, a video's credit scroll includes a long list of URLs. Another option is to include the list of sources in the online description of the video or on the wiki or blog page where the video is embedded as a part of a student's digital portfolio.

Creating Images and Videos

Students essentially have two choices: make the art or take photos. The options for creating art are endless. For taking photos, they should have access to a digital camera with at least a five megapixel lens and adequate memory. Many of them will have this tool available on their smart phones. A good flash and tripod are also useful. When taking pictures, they should apply the "rule of threes"—capture at least three images of the subject from different angles—as well as the "rule of thirds," where the focal point of the image is not the center of the picture, but on one intersection of a tic-tac-toe–style grid (and many cameras now have a feature to turn this grid on and off in the viewfinder). Subtle changes in lighting and the position of the subject may make a dramatic difference. Capturing video also requires the right equipment: a good video camera, a tripod, microphones, and adequate light (natural or artificial). For anything other than ambient, "B roll" footage, it is important to have steady, well-framed shots.

Creating Visualizations

Charts and graphs have long been a function in spreadsheet software such as Microsoft Excel. With tools like Google Docs, the process of creating visualizations has moved online, and students can build them using data they collect in real time. Many of the tools mentioned in the chapter on presentations can be used to create visuals for digital video texts. Panning across or zooming in on an infographic created with a tool like Infogram could provide both an interesting visual effect and share pertinent information with a viewer. Again, the thing to ask is whether the chart or graph is an appropriate, interesting, and not simply superfluous use of technology that contributes to this piece of digital writing.

Revising and Editing Digital Video Texts

In this important stage digital writers make final adjustments to their images, video clips, narration, timing, and other media elements. In many ways, this step is a kind of proofreading: making sure the meaning of the text is clear; adjusting the clips, transitions, and special effects; dotting the audio *i*'s and crossing the video *t*'s.

Multimedia composition invites students to use a number of effects to create an engaging text. We don't want our students to create digital videos that use bells and whistles—or worse, smoke and mirrors—to achieve fancy production values but, in the end, not really say anything about the subject at hand. The typical video production interface includes a variety of options that can add to, or detract from, the overall purpose and message students intend to create: titles, captions, transitions, sound effects, and filters, to name a few. Video-based genres have particular conventions to which they should adhere. For instance, we don't expect a television commercial to have a list of credits, but we certainly do expect a film to have such a list. We need to help students identify the genre they are working in, the conventions of that genre, and how best to help viewers understand the text they are creating in light of what they have previously seen and experienced in connection with that genre.

For instance, a student project about the obesity epidemic could be created in numerous ways. As an informational (and, to some degree, argumentative) text, a student might design a brief documentary in the same spirit as a film like *Super Size Me* (Spurlock 2004). To take a purely argumentative stance, the student might create a public service announcement in the form of a commercial. Another treatment of the subject might be a fictional narrative about a fellow student who works in a fast-food restaurant. Similar media could be created or collected for each of these projects, even though the presentation would vary. Students could even create a multimedia *and* multigenre project, exploring multiple genres and creating different videos for each. In any case, students should know and understand how the types of media they are collecting and creating will combine to many an effective video composition.

Publishing Digital Video

Multimedia work can be shared in many ways. Most of us immediately think of YouTube or Vimeo as spaces in which to publish digital video, both of which allow viewers to write comments in an accompanying discussion string, but many others exist. The web-based service VoiceThread (http://voicethread.com) provides unique opportunities, too. Students can post multimedia pieces next to which they—as well as other viewers—can embed text- or voice-based comments. Imagine the opportunities for students to reflect on their work. VoiceThread also allows students to create separate "pages" for different media components, and the viewer/reader can progress through the entire story, hearing different voices that have contributed to the piece. Sites like VideoANT (http://ant.umn.edu) allow users to post comments at the exact point in the timeline where they want to make a comment. Peers, parents, and we as teachers can comment on the way the writer uses a transition or effect at the point of occurrence, rather than having to describe that point in a comment posted separately.

All these services allow videos to be viewed from multiple platforms, including most mobile devices, and to be "embedded" in other websites. For instance, students can create a wiki page for their multimedia/multigenre project and then embed the final video into it. The video could also become one component of a "glog," essentially an online, interactive poster that students can create using Glogster (shown in Chapter 4). When using videos as part of a broader multimodal/multigenre project, students have to be sensitive to the overall design. If the video uses bright colors and snappy music, the accompanying website or glog should be designed in a similar manner, in order to reinforce the message.

Assessing Digital Video Texts

The broadest assessment consideration is that a story must be told, information must be presented, or an argument must be made. As with a written text, topic, structure, stance, and proper use of conventions should be evaluated. Whether a thirty-second public service announcement or a ten-minute minidocumentary, all video texts need to be produced in an intentional manner. Generally, viewers expect a beginning that catches their attention, a story developed through appropriate dialogue or narration, and effects judiciously used in service of the story or argument being made.

However, the ways in which a topic is introduced or elaborated on in a video may be different from the ways it would be in a formal essay or story. For instance, a person reading an essay or story would expect to see the title and author's name listed at the top of the text. In a video, there may be a title screen at the beginning or captions introducing the title and creator may appear a few moments in or the information may not come until the very end, depending on the effect the digital writer is hoping to achieve.

Also, as noted in *The Digital Writing Workshop*, we should value the process of composing a digital text (although certainly not at the exclusion of the product). In some ways, this is an obvious extrapolation of the reality that writing teachers evaluate writers in the process of writing. But it is difficult for students to document the process of composing a video (compared with automatically tracking changes in a word-processed document, for example). We should therefore look for evidence of brainstorming and revision in the way the timeline develops and changes, as well as for evidence that the student tried various techniques (sound effects, transitions) and sustained the message throughout. In short, what is it that you want students to know and be able to do as readers and writers, as speakers and listeners?

A few other assessment considerations for different genres include:

- Narrative:

  - How are characters introduced and setting established—with an image, verbal description, dialogue?

  - Is there a single narrator, or are multiple voices represented through dialogue?

  - What key media elements are included to propel the story forward, including transitions, sound effects, and music?

- Informational:

  - What framing shots are used to establish a context for the video and the credibility of the producer?

  - Is the narrator identified in the film or simply present as an anonymous voice-over?

  - How are new sources of information introduced? By other people? The narrator? Text? Images?

- Argumentative:

  - In what way is the tone of the argument established?

  - What information/statistics/sources count as evidence?

  - Is the video generally persuasive (relying more on rhetorical techniques) or argumentative (relying on reasoning and evidence)?

Finally, we can ask students to comment on their own work using tools like YouTube's annotations or VideoANT. Or we can ask them to prepare "director's cuts" in which, in screencasts they create using tools such as Jing or online services such as Screencast-O-Matic (www.screencast-o-matic.com) or Screenr (www.screenr.com), they describe their choices regarding the words they wrote, the images or clips they used, the effects they added, and so on. This work could be tied to a rubric they use to describe their own feelings about how they performed on the assignment overall. In so doing, they are again integrating all of the language arts while reflecting on the process of digital writing.

Examples of Student-Composed Digital Video Texts

The following examples do not include any narrative pieces—and not because I do not value narrative. Digital storytelling—combining one's own narration with images, music, sound, and sometimes video footage—has become an incredibly popular way to engage students in the digital writing process. I'm a strong proponent of digital storytelling and hear countless stories from teachers who use digital storytelling with great success in their classrooms. But the reality of the Common Core State Standards is that narrative will not be valued to the same degree as information and argumentation when it comes to assessment. Thus, the examples below are informational and argumentative in nature. While some could see this as capitulating to the standards or the tests, I hope what comes through clearly in these examples of informational/argumentative digital videos is the fact that students have been taught how to craft digital video texts with an effective introduction, a clearly developed main point, adequate details and examples, and an appropriate conclusion (and appropriate counterarguments in the case of argumentative writing). High-quality digital writing is creative, informed, and complete, regardless of the whims of any curricular fad, and skills learned with video can transfer back to more traditional writing processes.

With that in mind, and recognizing that narrative genres are also a viable option, the four example are

- The informational video "Plastic: Things You May Not Know," collaboratively composed by Elana Waugh's fourth graders in Leslie, Michigan.

- Two documentaries created by George Mayo's middle school students at the Silver Spring International Middle School, Maryland. The first is about refurbishing a school auditorium; the second is about the broader issues raised by America's war on drugs.

- An argumentative essay about illegal immigration created by Santos Hernandez, a student of Dawn Reed's in Okemos, Michigan.

Elementary: Informational Video Text

As part of a unit of study on ecosystems and the recursive nature of the water cycle, the students of Elana Waugh, a teacher at White Pine Academy, in Leslie, Michigan, produced a class book titled *Plastic: Things You May Not Know*. Waugh decided their work should be shared more widely and invited them to brainstorm, storyboard, script, and draw pictures for a video they would then enter in the Disney Planet Challenge Project contest. Please view the video (http://youtu.be/ESbYGpPk39o) and then read the analysis in Table 6.3 of the moves they made while crafting this piece of digital writing. As with other examples throughout this book, I encourage you to keep the MAPS heuristic in mind—mode, media, audience, purpose, and situation—to think about what these digital writers accomplished both individually and as a group.

Scan to view
Plastics video.

Returning to the broader view of MAPS, some of the main points to consider are how the students composed each page, as well as the overall piece. Throughout this video, the student narrators maintain a calm tone. Each segment is highly predictable: one sentence with each picture, followed by a transition into the next with consistent background music throughout. The final visual is a digital image of a pristine beach, perhaps taken by one of the students or a student's family member. As an informational text, this collaboratively composed video certainly does "examine a topic and convey ideas and information clearly" (CCSS). There is a clear introduction, as well as a clear conclusion, and sufficient details are used throughout, both in the narration and the images. As one way to compose an informational text, "Plastic: Things You May Not Know" accomplishes its goal of enlightening the reader while also providing a way for Waugh's students to collaborate and contribute to a broader digital project.

Documentary Video Texts

George Mayo, a teacher at Silver Spring International Middle School, Montgomery County, Maryland, brings craft principles into the process of creating documentary films. Over the course of a semester, he leads students in an inquiry that begins with questions from their own lives. These questions range from local interests to national issues and are always grounded in authentic research that will include interviews with experts, conducted in-person or via Skype video conferencing. George's students spend the entire semester exploring resources—both in print and online—and arranging to interview and record the experts. The process is highly recursive, involving many steps.

- Writing the script for the main body of the documentary in a voice that is both analytical and narrative; the issue must have a story behind it.

Table 6.3	Screenshots from *Plastic: Things You May Not Know*

Opening Screen

Over the opening visual, a narrator tells the title of the piece, and a few of Waugh's students say "plastic" in overlapping audio clips. As the video transitions to the first visual, the music fades. Keeping the MAPS heuristic in mind, I already begin to form some crafting questions. Since this was originally a book, I also wonder if a simulated page turn could have been a possible transition, too.

[title: *Plastic: Things You May Not Know*]

Demonstrating a Process: The Water Cycle

The first page of the "book," this visual on the water cycle, is accompanied by the first student narrator describing facts about water. While it might have been interesting to use a "Ken Burns" effect to follow the water cycle, having the camera pan backward to show all the places water exists on earth aligns with the statistics about how important water is to us as humans. The original image is shown again to make the point that the cycle is recursive, and this is all the water we have on earth.

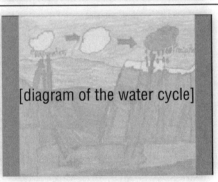
[diagram of the water cycle]

An Extended Definition of *Pollution*

About one minute into the video, a student offers a "dictionary" definition of pollution in conjunction with this image. In much the same way we would ask students to add details and examples to a traditional text, we next view images and accompanying narration about the different types of pollution that humans cause.

[drawing of people on a boat throwing trash overboard]

Table 6.3	**Screenshots from *Plastic: Things You May Not Know* (*cont.*)**
Image with Label At about ninety seconds into the video this image appears with the narration, "Pollution is one reason why we have endangered animals." The visual includes a label noting the plastic ring around the neck of a deer. Again, as I imagine the intended purpose and audience for this piece, I wonder if another animal would be effective in this picture.	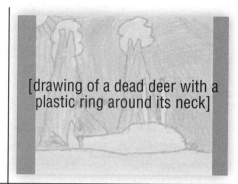 [drawing of a dead deer with a plastic ring around its neck]
Image with Caption In the original book, the text below the image was the main cue to the reader; the image was supplementary. The narrator of this particular segment reads the caption verbatim, and I do wonder how the students might have done something different with the narration in scenes like this, perhaps using it as an opportunity for a dialogue?	 [drawing of the Great Pacific Garbage Patch]
Chart Used to Illustrate a Statistic At about 2:40, a segment of the book states that 90 percent of the garbage patch in the Pacific Ocean is made of plastic. The subsequent section shows this chart indicating that 10 percent of all plastics end up in the ocean. Employing these percentages and creating the pie chart provide students an opportunity to practice their numeracy skills.	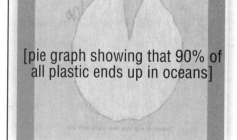 [pie graph showing that 90% of all plastic ends up in oceans]
Conclusion For all types of text, having an effective conclusion is key. At about 6:40 in the video, students begin listing the many things we can do to help slow the growth of the Pacific garbage patch. A few seconds before that, the narration introduces the slogan "reduce, reuse, recycle" and adds a fourth r: "refuse." This image, the first in their list of tips, supports the idea of refusing to use excessive plastic.	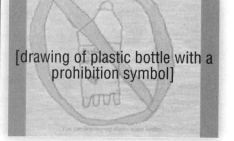 [drawing of plastic bottle with a prohibition symbol]

- Conducting research for about four weeks to develop questions, connections, and new ideas for interviews with experts.

- Conducting the interviews—either face-to-face or via Skype—and embedding transcribed portions into the script of their documentary film.

- Examining chunks of the written draft in conjunction with the video being edited.

George reports that the students come up with really good interview questions and the people being interviewed are often surprised by their quality. Even though George's approach to creating documentary films with his students requires a great deal of time, their commitment to the research process shows that there are lessons to be learned in how his students craft documentaries.

Before examining these two documentaries in depth, please browse the wiki on which students document their progress—http://studentdocs.wikispaces.com—to get a sense of the students' writing process. Then, watch the first video and read my analysis in Table 6.4.

Middle School: Informational/Argumentative Video 1
Saving the Old Blair Auditorium by Sarah Becker, Jason Bowie, Andrew Fuchs, Arielle Gottlieb, Hannah Rapp, and Jake Zastrow
(https://vimeo.com/42656751)

Scan to view Blair
Auditorium video.

This team of student filmmakers has created a documentary that is on par or even better than the stories you might see on a local television station. The lessons we can take from it for our own digital writers are many. First, having various kinds of evidence—from statistics to interviews to images to stories with personal appeal—is useful. The students make an effort to show both sides of the issue, even though the film ends with a plea for help on the auditorium project. Second, using a consistent pattern throughout—transitions with questions in a white font on a black background—is visually effective. The students also experimented with the idea of light and dark as Hannah moved about during the transitions between interviews. Finally, using actual documents and images related to the auditorium and its renovation, not random images found on the web, makes a much more convincing argument and shows the issue is still current. Together these techniques make this a

Table 6.4	Screenshots from *Old Blair Auditorium Student Documentary*

Guided by a consistent narrator, Hannah, the documentary begins in the Old Blair Auditorium. Hannah enters from stage right and says, "This is the Old Blair Auditorium. What would you say if you could save it?" She then provides some of the auditorium's history, as well as context for how it fell into disrepair when the high school transitioned into a middle school. This is an effective introduction to the overarching story they want to tell in this documentary.	
"But, during the move, one room was left untouched to rot and die away." The camera angle changes, and Hannah is now seen with her back to seats as the title sequence fades in. "This room is known as the Old Blair Auditorium." The still picture of the brightly lit auditorium is a stark contrast to the previous images and also invites us to see the view from the stage. We begin to understand the scope of what would need to be renovated.	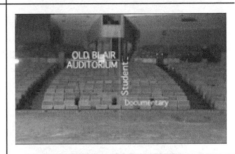
In the first of a number of transitions between segments of the video, a black screen presents this question: "What is wrong with the auditorium?" Subsequent sections are introduced with similar transitional screens. Each segment includes clips from interviews with the head of the community group supporting the renovation, a member of the county council, or the county executive.	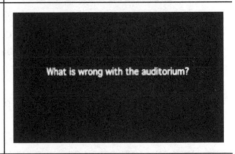
The segment describing what is wrong with the auditorium includes issues with the fire safety system, asbestos, and—as shown in this picture—the mold that has developed on the seats. Invited into the auditorium like this, we get a real sense of the damage present and what would be needed in order to renovate it. In cases like this, pictures really do speak louder than words. After about thirty seconds spent viewing the required renovations, the video switches to an interview clip.	

Table 6.4	Screenshots from *Old Blair Auditorium Student Documentary (cont.)*

The interview with Stuart Moore was filmed in a studio space the students created. Moore is positioned in the upper-left third of the screen (the "rule of thirds"). Valerie Ervin, a member of the county council, was interviewed in the same studio. The interview space is attractive, and the students ask good questions that elicit thoughtful responses.	
Hannah, seated in the auditorium for this segue, provides transitions between the interviews. Here she is describing why the project is not moving along and introducing County Executive Ike Leggett. Having Hannah sit rather than stand shows symbolically that the students are inviting conversation, not simply stating their demands.	
An on-location interview with Ike Legget, who explains the county's financial situation, follows. The students, as objective reporters creating a documentary film, allow him to speak for himself at length without interjecting. Like many politicians, he talks about things like "urgent needs" and doesn't really address the question directly. And they've captured it on film.	
Right before this final scene, Hannah talks about the financial status of the renovation. Even without a chart visually depicting the sharp disparity between existing and needed funding, the point is made clearly. Hannah's final narration begins while walking toward camera, stating, "We need *your* help to bring the Old Blair Auditorium back." She then exits stage right, a fitting ending that circles back to the initial image in the video.	

highly effective documentary and show that these students understand the craft of creating a digital video.

Middle School: Informational/Argumentative Video 2

The Drug War: Is It Time for a Change? by Solomon Bradford, Antonio Cardenas, Sam Elie, Shagufta Hussain, Ryan Smith, and Aaron Wilkerson (https://vimeo.com/43035730)

Scan to view Drug War video.

This student documentary is powerful for a number of reasons, the most important being that the young men creating it are in the population disproportionately targeted by America's war on drugs. The letter from former President Jimmy Carter and the interview with Dean Schmoke show that the students consulted high-level experts for information. While the video relies on repetitive tropes, returning to the letter and the interview a number of times, the narration moves things forward and, ultimately, offers alternatives to the war on drugs. These digital writers have certainly considered the issue's background, gathered appropriate evidence, and presented it in a compelling manner (see Table 6.5).

Both of these documentary films highlight how important it is for students to plan a video thoroughly if they want it to be of high quality. These projects took weeks to complete, but not all videos need to take that long. Nor should they. At the end of this chapter is a table that, much like the previous chapter on audio, looks at production value and time commitment in connection with various types of digital video projects. The type of commitment that Waugh's class project compared to Mayo's small group projects is worth noting too, especially as one more element in thinking about the situation component in MAPS: to what extent is the digital video project meant to be individualized as compared to collaborative? How much effort will students put forth in the editing and revision process compared to you as the teacher helping them organize their final projects? These are questions that only you can answer in the context of your classroom, curriculum, and students.

Also, consider the mode. Each of these three videos so far have been largely informational, with some persuasive elements. Do they effectively achieve the purpose of describing an idea? Certainly. Are they argumentative in the sense that they fully present counterarguments? Not necessarily. So, now, let's look at a video made by a high school student arguing his position on illegal immigration, and think about the techniques that he employs.

In this piece of student work and in others in this chapter, we have obscured images that the student used with a description of the images. While it is considered fair use for students to use copyrighted images for educational purposes, it is not fair use to print them in a book that is being offered for sale. For more information about fair use and copyright law, see page 9 of the introduction.

Table 6.5	Screenshots from *The Drug War: Is It Time for a Change?*

Many television news magazines or documentaries use a montage at the beginning. In the opening moments of their documentary, these students use this clip from C-Span and others showing money being printed and an overcrowded prison cell to illustrate the failure of the War on Drugs. These brief clips give us a preview of the topics they will discuss and their importance to the drug war.	 [speaker addressing Congress]
Music in the background carries an ominous tone, as kinetic type moves across the screen. Noting that drug consumption has risen by 34 percent over the past ten years (this fact is re-iterated later in the narration), the text then changes to the title, *The Drug War: Is It Time for a Change?* This title sequence was probably created automatically in a software program, but it shows that the students were zeroing in on particular facts important to their argument.	
The narrator, Sam Elie, introduces key points about the war on drugs after the initial montage. The students who worked on this film are mostly Latino and African American. Given the disproportionate effects of the drug war on these populations, the image of this young teen as a narrator is particularly powerful.	
After the initial clip of Sam talking, there is archival footage of President Nixon announcing that drug addiction is under control. This connects with the image of the present-day politician in the introductory montage and shows that the students are getting at the root of the issue. By blending different types of still and moving images, the students are visually demonstrating the scope of the drug war. The visuals support the scripted narration.	 [President Nixon speaking]

Table 6.5	Screenshots from *The Drug War: Is It Time for a Change? (cont.)*

The filmmakers zoom in, Ken Burns–like, on a screenshot of this article from Forbes.com, which highlights the fact that 62 percent of drug offenders are African American. Supporting one of the main subtexts of the documentary—that minorities are targeted in the drug war—with a statement in a reputable news source shows that the students have done research and are not just expressing personal opinions.	he War on Drugs is a War on Minorities and the Poor [article from Forbes: "The War on Drugs is a War on Minorities and the Poor"]
Prefaced with an image of Jimmy Carter, the videographers zoom in on a letter they received from President Carter, showing a close-up of the logo and date on the letter. Since an interview with President Carter would almost certainly have been impossible, using this letter as supporting evidence for their argument also demonstrates they are credible researchers.	JIMMY CARTER February 15, 2012
Here the students zoom in on a particular part of the letter, moving left to right as the narrator reads the top sentence. While seeing the words highlighted might have been more effective, that would have required more sophisticated software than the students had available. Still, the scrolling grabs our attention.	merican society suffers from a rtionately effects minorities, ar lent, I cautioned against creatir h people who are no threat to s g to an individual than the use l the lives of millions of young
After presenting information from the letter, the narrator introduces Kurt Schmoke, dean of the Howard Law School. There is an extended clip of him talking with two of the student researchers in a recorded Skype conversation. Schmoke speaks about the disproportionate incarceration rates for African Americans and Latinos, and it is clear he has the attention of his student interviewers.	

High School: Argumentative Video

http://youtu.be/r_1F21XrJXc

Scan to view
argumentative video.

This final example demonstrates a more direct approach than the previous three, distinctly argumentative in its form and tone. Throughout his narrated essay, Santos Hernandez balances a mix of statistics, historical facts, and present-day and historical images and uses different fonts to emphasize the points he is trying to make. At times, the images or captions on the screen say things for him that he doesn't wish to—or at least chooses not to—say out loud. At other points, the words that he speaks are echoed by the words on screen as if to emphasize the point. He precludes a number of counterarguments by offering statistics showing that illegal immigrants do, in fact, contribute to the American economy and that our nation's history of xenophobia is both long-running and bitterly ironic. While his video could be critiqued for the fact that he does not clearly present and refute counterarguments, one significant difference between Santos' digital writing and the other pieces above is that he takes a clearly provocative tone. His video provides us a good example for how to talk about the differences between—as well as the interrelation of—argumentative and persuasive techniques.

Given the current political discourse on cable news networks, is it any surprise that Santos composed his argumentative text the way that he did? Moreover, returning to MAPS, knowing that his audience is the general public, is he justified in taking this approach? These questions would be well worth considering in viewing his video as a mentor text, as well as other types of films that are presented as "documentaries" when shown in movie megaplexes (see Table 6.6).

What other lessons might we learn from these four video productions? The craft of digital writing in each case is certainly a process, whether individual or collaborative, short-term or long-term. Also, what does it mean for us to ask students to create a text from material they generate themselves rather than material they might find available online? A few ways to think about it are shown in Table 6.7.

Table 6.6	Screenshots from *Illegal Immigration*

With the music of Louis Armstrong's "A Kiss to Build a Dream On" playing in the background, the famous/infamous inscription from the Statue of Liberty opens the video. Then, over a time-lapsed video montage of the New York skyline at night, the narrator, Santos, outlines America's troubled history with immigration.	[text from the inscription on the Statue of Liberty]
Over film footage of immigrants on Ellis Island, as well as still images like the one to the right and political cartoons, Santos describes the ways people have been coming to the United States since the nation's inception. This particular screenshot makes the point that "undesirables" were excluded by the Page Act of 1875. As he speaks the word "Asians," it appears on screen in a different font color, followed by a question mark, indicating disbelief.	[photo of people circa 1875, with the words *Convicts*, *Prostitutes*, and *Asians*]
Over an image from a modern-day White House Easter egg roll, Santos describes the many types of "undesirables" that have been excluded from this country, whether because of race, nationality, or factors such as diseases or alcoholism. The respective words flash on the screen as he speaks. He cuts back and forth between archival footage and modern footage documenting many of the immigration reform acts of the twentieth century, ultimately leading to a fade-to-black transition about 2:30 into the video.	[photo of White House Easter Egg Roll with the word *Alcoholics*]
In the next segment, Santos describes current statistics about the estimated number of legal immigrants, the types of jobs they hold, and the effects on the American economy. (Since he produced this video in the spring of 2012, he also includes images of Barack Obama and Mitt Romney.) Over this image he states, "It is likely that the strawberries you are eating for lunch were picked by an illegal immigrant for well below minimum wage."	[photo of men tendiing crops]

Table 6.6	Screenshots from *Illegal Immigration (cont.)*

Critiquing current methods of immigration control, Santos includes a screenshot from YouTube of two girls climbing the border fence between the United States and Mexico. A number of other images, including pictures of border patrol agents detaining illegal immigrants, are shown in segment of the video as he highlights the costs involved annually and over the long term.	[photo of YouTube page with the title "Two girls climb US-Mexico border fence in less than 18 seconds"]
Over a two-minute discussion of how illegal immigrants contribute to the economy, Santos uses images from a press conference on May 19, 2010, featuring President Obama and Mexican President Calderon. Although Santos does not speak the words, this image of Obama at the White House superimposed with text makes it clear that Santos believes deportation is un-American.	[photo of President Obama, with the words *Deportation is UNAMERICAN*]
At about 7:15, another time-lapsed image of the sun setting provides a transition to a discussion of the Dream Act. Over numerous pictures of young immigrants marching and protesting, Santos' commentary describes the ways in which immigration reform could have beneficial outcomes for the United States but only if we act before it is too late (metaphorically, before the sun sets).	[photo of setting sun]
In the final moments of the video, Santos returns to the time-lapsed scene of New York, this time in daylight. He clearly understands the ways in which his video can be shared through social media and invites his viewers to "Be part of a revolution." This is a direct appeal to the viewer to do something before simply clicking off the video and moving to the next one in the YouTube queue, clearly understanding his audience and the media that they will be viewing.	[photo of city skyline, with the words *Be a part of the revolution* and the logos for Facebook and Twitter]

Table 6.7	Decisions Relative to Content Creation and Production Value for Video Texts	
	Lower Production Value	**Higher Production Value**
Higher Degree of Content Creation	■ Filming a scripted conversation/text with multiple voices ■ Using live action, but without costumes or on-location shots	■ Filming a multi-actor video, including original music, sound effects, and ambient ("B roll") footage ■ Using live action with careful attention to costumes, props, and lighting whether on a set or on location
Lower Degree of Content Creation	■ Filming an impromptu conversation or interview, perhaps with a mobile phone camera ■ Posting the video online with little or no additional editing	■ Filming a rehearsed conversation and using music or sound effects found online for added effect ■ Cutting between scenes, but otherwise performing minimal editing

Conclusion

At this point, you may be asking, is video production really a craft under the purview of writing teachers? This is so much work! In some ways, the process of crafting a digital video described in this chapter could, quite easily, be left to those in media production classes and ignored in a writing classroom. Our writing curriculum requires students to develop sentences, paragraphs, and essays; thus, creating thoughtful, high-quality video products is a labor-intensive process that would take away from the real work of writing instruction. Add the fact that access to the equipment and web-based resources students need to do this job well can be limited, so the task can become overwhelming both in terms of planning and implementation. I understand this and am sensitive to these concerns when colleagues share them with me. But as we think about why we should invite students to compose digital texts, I and others can offer at least three compelling reasons.

First, any kind of composing—whether print alone or any combination of media—requires a similar thinking process. The MAPS heuristic mentioned throughout this book requires us to help students think about how, when, and why they are producing messages for different audiences. While they may have mobile phones that allow them to record and share video, this fact alone does not necessarily make them competent composers of video texts. Digital writers need to think about the issues raised in this chapter in order to generate media that can be used subsequently in their multimedia projects. This is an act of crafting, not of simply recording.

Second, teachers generally report that students enjoy creating and sharing digital video projects, both with their peers in school and beyond the classroom. Of course, this in itself is not enough reason to invite students to create such projects. But, in tandem with thoughtful instruction and a focus on the digital writing process, digital video production is a multifaceted and productive process. Students will wrestle with making meaning on a number of levels, and they can think about how best to show certain aspects of their writing—through text, talk, image, sound, video, or some combination of these elements.

Third, at any point in the process of composing a multimedia text, we can invite students to pause and write about that process. Writing-to-learn is a proven strategy, and there is no reason we shouldn't have students reflect on their thinking and creativity along the way. This metacognitive approach allows students to talk about the connections they are making and push their ideas further—what is it they learn as they watch an interview for the third time or when they choose to reorder a series of images in their timeline?

The digital writing process, specifically creating video, could be seen as a superfluous add-on, a gimmick to get students excited to work on a research project or some other task. I encourage you instead to think about how your students can craft the video and still express themselves through writing—prewriting and drafting, in-process reflections, a final self-assessment—so that the text-based and media-based approaches work in conjunction with each other. Students will be conscious of their writing and thinking; viewing digital video as a means of composition can be a critical part of that process.

CRAFTING SOCIAL MEDIA | 7

In the connected age, reading and writing remain the two skills that are most likely to pay off with exponential results. Reading leads to more reading. Writing leads to better writing. Better writing leads to a bigger audience and more value creation. And the process repeats.

(Godin 2012)

Following an individual, company, or organization via social networking has become a standard part of our mass communication. Whether on Facebook, Pinterest, YouTube, FourSquare, or other services, we can find our friends, get deals, or simply "check in." One service in particular, Twitter, offers users the chance to answer a question: "What's happening?" Sharing status updates, photos, and links while playing games, instant messaging, or hanging out in a video-based chat room . . . it's all possible, whether from the smart phone in our palm or our desktop monitor. We can find and follow friends and strangers, experts and pundits. Each week the traditional media give us new numbers on social media: profits, users, trends. Social networks are becoming the way most people experience life online.

So, the ways in which we invite students to use social networks to share their own work and communicate with others matters a great deal. Merely signing on and posting a series of messages isn't tapping the possibilities of this socially networked digital writing practice. It's a case where text—having been born digitally—is experienced digitally. Simply reading a single tweet or even a series of tweets isn't nearly as important as participating in a conversation as Godin articulates.

In her *English Journal* article "Digitalk as Community" (2012), Kristen Turner reminds us of the world in which our students live and its stark contrast to their literacy experiences in school.

> *In the digital world adolescents choose the communities to which they belong; they decide to what extent they will engage in the norms of those communities; they determine the level of language play that will mark their individual identities. In school, however, this power to choose often does not exist, and tasks assigned have little value to teens beyond the assessment. (40)*

While it is difficult for those of us who are still catching up with the latest social media craze to think of all the possibilities for using it in our classrooms, Turner's main point—that the literacy practices our students use outside school to form community don't typically exist inside school—indicates that we must rethink why and how we are using digital writing tools in our classrooms.

And, whether we feel the changes are good ones or not, they are already here. In an Edutopia blog post, Steve Johnson (2010) suggests the following reasons teachers should advocate using social media:

- It is quickly becoming our duty as educators in the twenty-first century to guide our students toward responsible use of social media.
- Social media use is becoming our new first impression.
- Connected, community-based learning is important.
- In five years, the filters will be gone whether we like it or not.

He goes on to elaborate reasons teachers should support students as they learn cyber citizenship. And remember, he posted this years ago.

The flip side is that social media have many negatives. Numerous instances have occurred of an employee losing a job over an errant photo or status update. Stalkers, cyberbullies, spammers, viruses, and other invasions to our privacy come as a consequence of living life online. While I believe our culture focuses too much on the negative aspects of social media, often while ignoring the positives, there are risks that keep educators from using social media as tools for teaching digital writing. As a result, we as teachers don't know how to use social media in fluid ways, and students are not thinking about the consequences of their digital footprint. Grabill's survey of college freshmen reveals that most of them don't even view social networking and texting as *writing* (MSU News 2010), and thus we have a unique contribution to make to their learning. Without taking all the fun out of social media, we can help students be more intentional in the ways they employ these tools to link to online resources, comment on others' status messages, and contribute to the wider discourse on what they value in their lives.

In thinking about why and how our students engage in social media, a recent extensive ethnographic study shows that young people participate in online activities in varying degrees, from hanging out to messing around to geeking out (Ito et al., 2009). Each type of participation includes different levels of engagement

- *Hanging out*—participating in social media, watching videos, and casual web surfing

- *Messing around*—playing games informally and designing websites or other online materials

- *Geeking out*—creating high-quality remixes, fully participating in online gaming

Depending on what youth aim to do online—and how they act as digital writers in doing it—they are constructing identities, building (or destroying) relationships, creating new opportunities for learning, and remixing various digital media to produce new compositions such as blogs, wikis, and videos. I maintain that applying the lenses of craft when using social media will help students in this process. MAPS still matters, even if the writing comes quickly. Slowing down just long enough to think through a text message, status update, or tweet—and thinking about audience, purpose, and situation—helps them be responsible, present a good first online impression, and participate actively in a variety of communities.

Noted earlier, Howard Rheingold reminds us that attention matters. His contemporary, Cathy Davidson, in *Now You See It: How the Brain Science of Attention Will Transform the Way We Live, Work, and Learn* (2011), describes a number of conceptual shifts that we as educators need to make in order to adapt to new ways of paying attention. She argues that our attention to multitasking is missing the point, and that there is something more important to consider.

What we haven't done yet is rethink how we need to be organizing our institutions—our schools, our offices—to maximize the opportunities of our digital era.

We're so busy attending to multitasking, information overload, privacy, our children's security online, or just learning the new software program and trying to figure out if we can really live without Twitter or FourSquare, that we haven't rethought the institutions that should be preparing for more changes ahead. (12)

As I frame the craft of writing social media in this chapter, I want to reiterate the fact that our main goal is to help students become intentional. If we simply have students sign up with a social media service and then use it in the same way we use other web-based tools—distribute assignments, have students randomly reply to each other in discussion posts—we are not inviting them to think deeply and creatively about how to craft social media texts. If we only use social media to re-create teacher-centered instruction, we're not using its power to our students' advantage.

Social media is the telephone for this generation of teens (and, increasingly, adults). We struggle with recognizing social media as an example of digital writing because so much of what students produce is meant for their own amusement or centered on building relationships. This is not bad, though: We want our children to be well-rounded, communicative people. Still, Wilhelm (2010) cautions us to focus on the way we communicate with students and invite them to communicate with one another.

For that matter, we should always ask if what we are doing in school is something that requires community, if it fulfills the unique possibilities of people working together on a common project that leads the participating individuals to independence. If it is something that only requires technology, and not a coming together over a shared inquiry and conjoint experience, then we have not fulfilled the unique potential of that place we know as school. Technology can help us to fulfill that potential, but it can also lead us away from it. (46)

Our uses of social media are only as powerful as the teaching that supports these uses. We can create a space for students to post comments and share links, but does that in and of itself build community in our classrooms? Certainly not. Social networks, are composed of people. And these people need to be nurtured, their networks created as safe and welcoming spaces. Examining Twitter offers us one way to do just that.

Viewing a Professional Mentor Text: Tweets

Even though Twitter has only a fraction of the number of users other social networks have, its impact on conversations between people around the world with common interests has been significant. In 140 characters, we can offer a status update (the classic, "what I ate for breakfast," is one that often garners criticism), comment on the latest political gaffe, or, more importantly, engage in a professional conversation. Twitter, as a microblogging platform, offers digital writers a variety of opportunities and constraints. As Mills and Chandra (2011) describe it

> *Unlike conventional forms of print-based writing, which readers cannot modify, microblogging is characterized by rapid interactivity between authors and readers. There was a quality of transparency and immediacy among users as their writing was distributed to a peer audience within moments of its construction. The activity required engagement with existing content in the thread to further improve upon it. We observed that microblogging threads are not static, discrete units, but are dynamic and malleable, open to reauthoring multiple times. (39)*

They go on to outline features of microblogging. Three are of particular note.

- Following microblogging posts frequently involves both multidirectional and linear pathways. Users insert hyperlinks to create multidirectional pathways, while entries follow a sequence that is ordered by time.

- Microblogging reflects upon itself [it is metadiscursive] as authors comment on previous posts in the thread.

- Microblogging involves a rapid and transparent process of text creation and distribution. Once posted, entries are quickly followed by feedback. (42)

The art and skill of composing something as seemingly simple as a tweet is more than simply typing a limited number of characters into a small box. Nevertheless, the craft a digital writer employs to design a Twitter message, which is both technical and rhetorical, is aimed at brevity. There are a few ways to make that happen, even in 140 characters, if we understand our audience and the situation for the tweet.

For me, the most important part of how I frame a tweet is the way it ultimately shows up on a user's screen, thus I include hashtags—a word preceded by the # sign that will show up quickly in Twitter searches—and sometimes even direct my tweets to a specific other user using "at replies" by mentioning another user with the @ sign and his or her Twitter handle. If I want to share something longer than 140 characters, I could write a blog entry and promote it in a tweet that (1) indicates I have written a blog post, (2) gives some indication of the topic, and (3) provides a link (a shortened one courtesy of the app I use to manage my Twitter account, HootSuite [http://hootsuite.com]). Then I send it to the appropriate Twitter users and communities, usually the National Writing Project (#nwp), National Council of Teachers of English (#ncte), and the Twitter chat groups for #literacies and #engchat. This way, I am making my tweet available not only to users that subscribe to me as followers, but also to anyone who is following these various streams related to teaching English. An example of a "final draft" of my tweet is shown in Figure 7.1.

Another interesting aspect of Twitter is that it can be amplified by a variety of web-based services such as Storify (http://storify.com) and Paper.li (http://paper.li), as well as apps such as Flipboard (http://flipboard.com) and Zite (http://zite.com), which can turn your Twitter stream into an ever-evolving magazine on your iOS or

Figure 7.1

My Tweet About the CRWP Open Institute

Troy Hicks @hickstro   15 Jul
New blog post: "Reflections on CRWP 2012 Open Institute"
ow.ly/cfPDK #nwp #ncte #literacies #engchat
Expand

Android device. Most of my tweets include links (either to my own work or other items that I have found interesting), so when these tweets run through Flipboard my readers get a preview. My tweet in Figure 7.1—quite plain in the Twitter interface—in Flipboard looks like the screenshot in Figure 7.2. On the left, you can see all my recent tweets in a visually appealing layout. Then, by clicking on any one particular tweet, it expands to show the entire post on my blog. Flipboard, thus, offers me a convenient way to keep track of the many items that colleagues in my Twitter network are sharing.

Groups of Twitter users regularly converse with one another through "at replies" (the @ symbol with a user's name), direct messages, and hashtag conversations—those held by Meenoo Rami's #engchat group, for example. Started in the fall of 2010 as a way for English teachers to connect via Twitter, the #engchat group

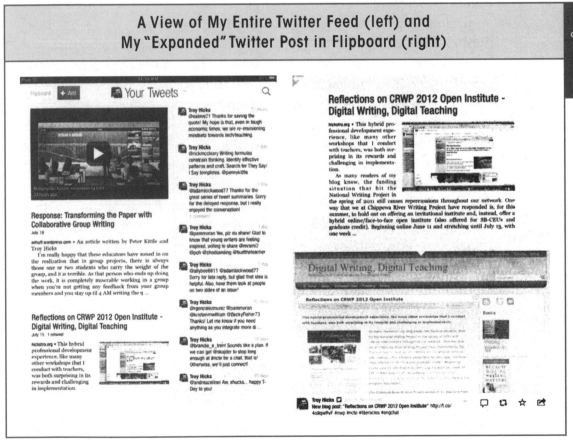

A View of My Entire Twitter Feed (left) and My "Expanded" Twitter Post in Flipboard (right)

Figure 7.2

typically meets on Monday nights at 7:00 p.m. EST and invites different educators to act as "host" each week. For example, I hosted an #engchat conversation on January 3, 2011 (http://goo.gl/pjM27) and cohosted with Franki Sibberson on April 23, 2012 (http://goo.gl/P9Zhq), and again with colleagues Sara Kajder, Bud Hunt, and Carl Young on May 21, 2012 (http://goo.gl/iWa0x). These conversations can have dozens, if not hundreds of participants and are in many ways a series of instant messages. All the participants use the hashtag #engchat in their messages and have a separate stream set up where they can read incoming messages. Conversations are fast, and much gets discussed in these sixty-minute bursts. As noted above, using a tool such as HootSuite allows me to keep track of the conversation much easier than simply trying to pick out and reply to individual tweets in my entire Twitter stream. Still, as noted many times, intention matters, and the way that I craft these brief pieces of digital writing must have some certain elements in order to move the conversation forward.

Figure 7.3 presents a selection of tweets from my #engchat conversation on April 23, 2012, after one of the participants, Ben Kuhlman, posed a question related to units of study for digital writing. Note the time of Ben's first tweet at 7:03 and the last at 7:14. In those eleven minutes, there were fifty-eight other tweets sent to the #engchat stream from eighteen different people, one of whom was someone simply using the hashtag to make an announcement, not participate in the chat. I pull out this specific series of interactions across that time frame between Ben and I as an example of how we could communicate with one another directly, yet still contribute to the broader dialogue of that #engchat conversation. Notice how we both use @ replies to signal a question or response for one another and the hashtag to keep the conversation in the same stream. You can see that he and I were both thinking general thoughts about studying digital genres and our tweets essentially crossed in the stream. Yet, in his final tweet, Ben replied directly to my question by addressing me with the @ reply.

One final note about engaging in social media as a professional educator: We can (and according to many experts, should) enter the conversation. Analyze. Discern. Inform. Participate. These are the possibilities for digital writers as they explore uses of social media. There so many great bloggers to read, tweeters to follow, and social networks to participate in that I won't even try to list them. Instead, my suggestion for getting started is to sign up for email alerts from professional organizations, including NCTE's Inbox (www.highroadsolution.com/

A Conversation Exchange on #engchat

Figure 7.3

 bkuhl2you #engchat I'm interested in what people have done with digital genres and any online genres/units for Katie Wood Ray–esque "Units of Study" –7:03 PM Apr 23rd, 2012

 hickstro @bkuhl2you Thinking about "units of study" for digital texts is interesting. On the one hand, they deserve time and attention alone. **#engchat** –7:06 PM Apr 23rd, 2012

 bkuhl2you #engchat I tried teaching a very short unit about the genre of the Tweet, but it didn't get very far – not sure if it was me or the students –7:06 PM Apr 23rd, 2012

 hickstro @bkuhl2you In another sense, "digital" texts are just as much a part of what we do as "analog" texts. How/when do they not fit in? **#engchat** –7:06 PM Apr 23rd, 2012

 bkuhl2you @hickstro #engchat When other teachers don't teach them, and when students aren't using them. Then I'm introducing the technology. –7:14 PM Apr 23rd, 2012

---

ncte_preference_center/Form.aspx), NCLE's SmartBrief (www.smartbrief.com/ ncle/index.jsp), and Edutopia (www.edutopia.org/edutopia/enews). There are more of course, but these three resources will help you discover great writing and technology resources, begin following RSS feeds, find great tweeters, and get involved in social networks.

Exploring the Digital Writing Process for Social Media

Common Core Anchor Writing Standard 6 ("Use technology, including the Internet, to produce and publish writing and to interact and collaborate with others") is proof that technology is influencing the teaching of writing. As students compose texts, social media help them develop ideas, give and receive feedback, and ultimately share their work with a worldwide audience.

Prewriting and Drafting Social Media

Returning to MAPS, the situation of social media is particularly relevant. One of the main challenges is that exchanges on social media happen quickly. If our idea is to make it into the social media arena with the rest of the ideas about a topic, there is barely enough time to type it, let alone be witty and insightful or raise some attention-getting hackles.

Being intentional with the writing, we need to ask: What is the purpose of the message? A social media post can be either the final step in the process of composing digital writing or a first and only step in sharing something "cool." My hope is that you invite your students to share their work with their peers and the world, not push the content of others. Certainly, there will be appropriate occasions when students may want to "retweet," post, share, or comment on someone else's work (preferably a unique piece of digital writing by a classmate or other peer). But for the most part, I urge you to have your students create significant texts—like the ones described in previous chapters—and share links to their work, inviting feedback from their classmates and perhaps beyond the classroom as well.

The prewriting process for a social media post happens well before a student logs in to Twitter, Pinterest, or some other service. An argumentative blog post, a contribution to an informational wiki page, or a digital story uploaded to a video site is really the final step in the composing process. Posting the piece and then sending out a link to it via text message is an invitation for response.

Choosing a Social Media Platform

The concepts presented in this book related to composing web-based texts, presentations, audio texts, and video texts are likely to stay relatively constant despite new technologies that emerge. Social media, however, change every day. The creators of Twitter never imagined the hashtag as a way to track information on their service, but as I write this chapter in the late summer of 2012, the "#Olympics" hashtag is applied to millions of tweets per day.

Choosing a platform will likely be as much about your school's acceptable-use policy as about your pedagogical goals. Even though many users of social media are younger than thirteen, laws in the United States limit users from signing up for many web-based services until that age. Certain sites and services allow teachers to sign up for accounts and add students without email-address verification. As you work with your colleagues, principal, and technology coordinator, I encourage you to explore the Consortium for School Networking's *Acceptable Use Policies in the Web 2.0 and Mobile Era* (Consortium for School Networking 2011). Among their reasons for reevaluating acceptable-use policies on a regular basis: "Given the increasing extent of use of cell phones and other mobile technologies by students, the need for formal policy pertaining to personally owned mobile devices is clear."

Social media platforms do come and go quickly (despite the seeming dominance of Facebook), and they're not all the same. Table 7.1 briefly outlines a few features from some of the major ones, but by the time this book goes to press, there will be more. I encourage you to join the wiki group related to this book and contribute your ideas as new tools become available: http://digitalwritingworkshop .wikispaces.com/Websites_And_Apps.

Scan to view websites and apps.

Revising and Editing Social Media

Social network posts are often first draft thinking in final draft form. Revising and editing have to happen before the message is sent, and we usually don't take (or don't always have) the time. Still, we can certainly invite our students to think carefully about what they are posting and why. For instance

- Are you creating a new message to begin a thread, or are you replying to someone else? How will your readers know what you are doing?

- Depending on where and with whom you were sharing the social media message, is it appropriate to be sarcastic or witty? Is it appropriate to use abbreviations or texting lingo?

- If you are including a link, will your readers find your own original content or content you are sharing from another source? What is your purpose for sharing this content?

- Assuming that you want feedback to one of your own digital writing products, in what ways have you participated in the community with whom you

Table 7.1	An Overview of Social Media Tools for Digital Writing		
	Twitter	**Edmodo**	**Cel.ly**
Format	*Microblogging:* characterized by short messages (140 characters), the use of "@" replies, and "#" hashtags	*Social networking:* characterized by Facebook-like status updates with links and embedded media	*Group text messaging:* characterized by the ability to send messages directly to a user's cell phone
Possible Purposes	■ Engaging in conversation, especially with "@" replies to individuals or "#" hashtags to groups ■ Very brief summaries of texts ■ Sharing short quotes, with attribution ■ Linking to other content the student has produced ■ Adopting the persona of a character and tweeting as that character	■ Creating individual profiles with links to "likes" and samples of work ■ Extended discussions on class topics or links to outside resources ■ Creating and sharing resources in a class space ■ Connecting with other classes in a shared space	■ Sending out reminders to students with links to homework or other class information ■ Engaging in a class discussion via text message ■ Taking a real-time poll in class ■ Having students share links to examples of real-world, digital texts as they encounter them
Similar Tools	■ Google+ ■ Plurk ■ Tumblr ■ Vibe	■ Schoology ■ Twiducate	■ Kik ■ iMessage (iOS)

are sharing your work? Have you offered high-quality comments and feedback to others?

■ If you are using social media to collaborate, have you and your group members agreed on some norms for posting materials? For instance, if you are curating a shared board of links for your research project, how will you evaluate sources before posting them publicly?

Table 7.1	An Overview of Social Media Tools for Digital Writing (*cont.*)

	Diigo	**Today's Meet**	**Scoop.it**
Format	*Social bookmarking:* characterized by saving URLs across devices, with the ability to share links with other users	*Backchanneling:* characterized by participants taking notes, asking questions, and posting related links during a presentation or discussion	*Content curation:* characterized by saving links to existing content, usually presented as a web page
Possible Purposes	■ Developing a group around common interests to share and comment on links ■ Using features such as "sticky notes" to annotate and have discussions on web pages ■ Subscribing to the bookmark feeds of experts and other students interested in a topic	■ Inviting students to brainstorm ideas or generate a list of questions before a presentation or discussion ■ During a discussion, inviting students to compliment others on a well-stated point or cogent argument ■ Sharing links to relevant sources of information discussed ■ After a discussion, rereading the transcript and summarizing ideas	■ Working individually or in small groups, have students create curated collections of high-quality content about a topic ■ Add commentary and response to found content ■ Develop own content and curate it into a collection ■ Follow the collections of others and offer constructive feedback
Similar Tools	■ Delicious ■ Google Bookmarks ■ Pocket	■ Co-Meeting ■ HootCourse	■ Pinterest ■ MentorMob

Although this list of questions is not a guaranteed way to ensure that social media messages will be relevant and engaging, it should help start a conversation with your students about why and how they are using these digital writing tools. Once a social media message is posted—even if the system allows you to subsequently delete it—someone will probably see it immediately. Perhaps it is time to reformulate Benjamin Franklin's classic advice for the digital age: a pixel of prevention is worth many messages of cure.

Example of Student-Created Social Media Texts: Youth Voices

One final example of students using social media in effective ways comes from a source that I shared in *The Digital Writing Workshop*, and continues to be a model community for digital writing. The Youth Voices network was begun nearly a decade ago by Paul Allison, a teacher in New York City, and has included dozens of teachers and hundreds of students over the years. The common theme in all the writing shared via Youth Voices is that students create interest-driven, thoughtfully composed pieces. Sometimes the writing comes in the form of a blog post, sometimes as an image, or even recorded as a podcast. Across all the writing, students are coached to create strong pieces and shown smart ways to offer response to one another.

Scan to view
Andrew's post.

One recent example (http://goo.gl/EGVxL) demonstrates how an initial post from Andrew, shown Figure 7.4 , then led to broader conversations. Worth noting here, Andrew's initial post is well researched, and clearly states his position. This is writing that he is sharing while in the process of researching the war on drugs, and he shares it on Youth Voices so other students were then able to reply, both by commenting positively on his writing and by asking questions or raising concerns. The Youth Voices website (http://youthvoices.net/guide/archives) has an extensive collection of response guides that students use as templates for replying to one another in thoughtful, constructive ways. Andrew did receive some feedback, and it made him think and write more.

For instance, Figure 7.5 is Andrew's reply to Christopher, who had suggested that legalizing drugs would bring unintended consequences. Andrew doesn't use the standard "Re:" as a response, instead titling it "respectfully." And he not only offers a counterargument but also supports this claim with a hyperlink to relevant evidence. In terms of both argumentative skill and effective use of technology, Andrew's reply is exceptionally thoughtful. As Andrew moves from posting on his blog to developing a more complete argumentative essay, these interchanges with his classmates as well as other students from around the country will help him craft a stronger piece of writing.

Figure 7.4

Andrew's Initial Post

Why I Think the War on Drugs Needs to End

DISCUSSION   Feb 24, 2012

by: andrewa

keywords   ◆ america ◆ end ◆ failure ◆ war on drugs

channels   ◆ literature and inquiry

America's War on Drugs has been a huge failure. It has caused much more harm than good since it started nearly 40 years ago when President Nixon created the Drug Enforcement Administration. I really want people to understand the fact that I am not condoning the use of drugs, but that waging a war on drugs has been more costly to society than drugs itself.

It has cost America $2.5 trillion dollars over the last 40 years and it has produced many unnecessary casualties. Organized crime has arisen because of the illegality of drugs, much like it did in the 1920s when America prohibited the use of alcohol. People still found a way to get alcohol during the Prohibition, and the same is happening now with drug prohibition.

Despite the US cracking down harder then ever before on drug laws, people are still finding a way to get drugs, and with this they are fueling the organized crime that drug dealers thrive on. I think it is really important to stop treating petty drug offenders as criminals and start treating them as human beings who need medical help to overcome their addictions.

For years alcoholics have been treated with programs like AA, because alcoholism truly is a problem that requires external help for the addict. Drug addicts should be treated the same way because it would do so much more good to send a drug addict to a treatment facility then it would to send them to jail.

The war on drugs needs to end now because it is a war that will never be won.

Paul Allison, the teacher who coordinates Youth Voices, uses www.twitterfeed .com to automatically create tweets announcing new posts (see the example in Figure 7.6). What are some of the elements that make this message eye-catching? The tweet is essentially the first sentences from Andrew's post, what I imagine to be a

Figure 7.5

Andrew's Response to Christopher

respectfully

Submitted by andrewa on Wed, 2012-03-07 14:07.

Christopher I understand what you are saying here but you should realize that Portugal decriminalized all drugs 10 years ago, despite heavy opposition, and the results have been great. Drug addiction rates have gone down, incarceration rates have gone down, and drug use has gone down. Instead of being sent to jail for drug possession, offenders in Portugal are referred to drug treatment facilities and there are solid numbers and evidence that drug related crimes and addictions have gone down. I expect a similar outcome if the same were to happen in the United States.

http://www.time.com/time/health/article/0,8599,1893946,00.html

reply

Figure 7.6

Twitter Message Announcing Andrew's Blog Post

 youthvoices America's **War** on **Drugs** has been a huge failure. It has caused much more harm than good since it started nearly ... http://t.co/VJlkdoYC

9:21 PM Feb 24th from twitterfeed

function of TwitterFeed. Given the number of posts that Allison would have to share each day, automation is probably a smart move. However, might you as a digital writer have crafted something more interesting for your Twitter followers? Instead of simply picking up the first sentence, how could you use 140 to invite readers into clicking on the link to your blog post?

Conclusion

Part of the benefit of a social network is the ease it provides to be, well, social. Another part of the benefit of social networks is that they allow a writer to create a living archive of work. While this could become a bit overwhelming as you work with students to help them figure out what to post where, as well as how to do it, combining both can be beneficial, as students create their own identities as writers, and responders, across digital spaces. Basically, they create a public, digital footprint with their writer's profile that continues to grow into a portfolio, and they learn cyber citizenship by participating in the class's social network in productive ways. With both, we invite students to craft substantive texts with digital writing tools and then ask them to share their work in clear, succinct manner through social media.

A social network profile and a writers' broader online profile certainly overlap, but though the two spaces are complementary, they are separate. While a social network profile would be specific, and could be made private, the broader online profile of a student that someone finds from using a web search could reveal any number of writings, pictures, or other media. As we think about how to help students participate responsibly, represent themselves ethically, and develop an overall online persona, social networking can be one part of the broader digital writing toolset. By thinking about how digital writers work over time by modeling and mentoring them through the writing process, we can help them create strong digital footprints. The final chapter invites us to think about how to teach our digital writers to do just that.

MODELING AND MENTORING THE DIGITAL WRITING PROCESS

began my first book, *The Digital Writing Workshop*, by saying, "Like you, I am a teacher of writing." Many of the teachers with whom I have worked over the past few years have told me how powerful they find this statement. Even though the technologies may change, at the core we are still writers. To prove that point, throughout this book I have identified and analyzed the decisions students have made when crafting digital writing, returning to the MAPS heuristic of mode, media, audience, purpose, and situation. Media reports and uninformed opinions may continue to belittle our youth and call them dumb or shallow. Or, as I hope you've come to understand, I believe we can use what we know about craft to help them become better writers, employing a variety of digital tools given the context for their work. And writers today have more possibilities than ever.

We are also living in an era in which mobile devices and increasing access to the Internet provide our students (at least outside school) with countless opportunities to produce and consume content for wider and wider audiences. Do students write everything, all the time, with intention and creativity? No. Careless status messages or hastily taken pictures have caused youth (and adults, for that matter) to regret what they have composed in digital spaces. Nevertheless, Mills (2010) summarizes an argument made by many of us who are convinced we need to integrate technology into writing instruction.

> *Teachers of English need to do more than incorporate the out-of-school literacy practices, interests, and predilections of youth. They must also extend the range of multimodal practices with which students are conversant. Teachers can extend the multimodal literacies that are valued in youth networks to give students recognition in the global communications environment. (42)*

However, the data and experience of educational leaders and the thousands of teachers in classrooms every day tell us that if anything is going to change, it needs to happen in classroom interactions between teachers and students. At the same time, we have been beleaguered by a number of challenges, including the continued devastating cuts to funding for public education, new federal funding models that force us into competition rather than collaboration, and increased scrutiny from consortia creating new standards and assessments. Just because more of our writing is moving online does not mean we can sacrifice the relationships we have with our writers.

Instead, we need to see the increasing ease of use and compatibility of web-based writing tools as a new means of producing digital writing, one that will both meet Common Core State Standards and engage writers.

> *The changes described by our colleagues in the early days of the 21st century do matter. They matter a great deal because, quite simply, the technology has evolved to a point where social practices—ours and, more importantly, our students'—are changing in ways that we cannot hide from in school. The fact that we (and our students) are now able to hold a device in our pockets that allows us to read and annotate an original text, stream (on demand) multiple film adaptations of the text, look at the SparkNotes about the text, and find essays about the text from online paper mills—all at the flick of a finger—is significant.*
>
> *Or, at least, it* feels *significant. (Hicks, Young, Kajder, and Hunt 2012, 72)*

In this final chapter, I first respond to what I call FAQs, or "frequently argued questions." When teachers ask me these questions, I know they are doing so out of frustration and with the best of intentions. I phrase and answer the questions the way I do because we can no longer rely on the questions as a crutch, as an excuse not to teach digital writing. My hope is that these questions and my responses will quell your own fears and also help you become a stronger advocate for digital writing. While I understand that some classrooms, schools, and communities are still dealing with a very serious digital divide, I also believe that these are the types of skills that we need to teach our students not only for college and career success, but so they can be thoughtful and respectful communicators throughout their lives.

The second part of this chapter examines a portfolio of student work through the lens of the previously mentioned document titled *Framework for Success in Post-secondary Writing*, which focuses on "habits of mind" and the "ways of approaching learning that are both intellectual and practical" (Council of Writing Project Administrators, National Council of Teachers of English, and National Writing Project 2011, 4). My assessment considers these habits of mind in the context of the particular skills demanded in the Common Core State Standards. The student, Lydia Touchette, is a sixth grader in Kevin Hodgson's class at Norris Elementary School, in Southampton, Massachusetts. The combination of Kevin's innovative teaching and Lydia's creativity gives us a glimpse into how these "habits of mind" are fostered through the craft of digital writing. While it may be a stretch for some readers to agree with all parts of Kevin's pedagogical approach as "teaching writing" (especially his emphasis on game theory), Lydia's portfolio provides a model of what we want students to produce in our digital writing workshops. Finally, we will peek at my own son's digital portfolio as a way to think about synthesizing the many ideas in this book.

FAQs: Frequently Argued Questions About Digital Writing

1. All this digital stuff is cool, but what about "real writing" and what it means to compose academic texts? How do we prepare kids for college and a career?

As a result of the misplaced motivations of billionaire businessmen and an educational testing industry run amok, we now find ourselves with core standards that value argumentative writing over informational writing and informational writing over narrative. We know that students will be assessed by writing produced for computer-based tests, tests that are convenient for automated scoring. However, even though our children are being forced into more constricted writing genres, we still have the opportunity to teach writing well.

The Common Core State Standards have laid out a distinct set of the skills students should know and be able to exercise. The *Framework for Success in Postsecondary Writing*, in establishing "habits of mind," offers us insights on how we can accomplish these goals. Combining our vision of what students "should" do when they're writing with what they *could* do is incredibly important. We need to overcome what my colleague Anne Whitney (2011) calls the "schoolishness of school" and invite our students to produce authentic writing.

We can do this without resorting to old tropes. A group of my colleagues from CMU has researched what college professors want from their student writers.

> *EJ readers may be interested to learn that not one professor mentioned five-paragraph essays or "traditional" high school research papers in the focus group discussions as essential in college writing. Not as a standard academic form. Not as a stepping stone. Not as an organizational strategy. (Brockman, Taylor, Kreth, and Crawford 2011, 76)*

In other words, it is time to give up on the idea that we are doing students a service by limiting the range of writing experiences we offer. We need to get beyond our conceptions of writing as a set, linear process with predictable outcomes. We need to embrace the messiness of writing. Digital tools can help us do that in more robust, creative, and efficient ways than we have ever had available before as writing teachers. Embracing digital writing will, in the end, support all our writers both in their academic careers and in their lives.

2. Grammar is crucial, so what do we do about "txting" in students' formal writing?

No formal study has shown that "txting" ruins students' writing. Plester, Wood, and Bell (2008), in a study of eleven- and twelve-year-olds, conclude that "there is no evidence that knowledge of textisms by pre-teen children has any negative association with their written language competence, which contrasts with the bulk of the media coverage." Texting lingo, or "digitalk" as my colleague Kristen Turner describes it, in student papers should not alarm us; we just need to help students understand when and how to use different discourses for social and school purposes (Turner 2012). By inviting students to think about different audiences and purposes for their writing, we can help them identify when they should and should not use certain forms of language. Robb (2010), for instance, invites students to craft text messages as an alternative to typical school writing. There may be times when texting lingo is more appropriate—a passage where two teens are communicating, for example. Don't throw texting out; recognize it as a way of code switching and teach student appropriate ways to move back and forth between formal and informal discourses.

3. Aren't we circumventing the research process by using all these digital tools?

Sadly, unscrupulous students have always found ways to circumvent the process of doing research. In blog posts, journal articles, and books, as well as conference presentations and informal discussions, many of the experts I trust suggest that digital research tools can, in fact, improve research. Students can now participate in more complex, well-reasoned, and personalized research than has ever been possible. (For continual reassurance of this fact, I strongly recommend checking Joyce Valenza's blog—http://blog.schoollibraryjournal.com/neverendingsearch— for her latest thinking and the newest tools.)

If you're not convinced by the growing chorus of educators who advocate using digital writing tools, consider this: Years of research have shown that if your students are engaged in authentic inquiry, writing about topics they have chosen, and sharing their ideas with like-minded (and sometimes non-like-minded) peers, they will be creating smart writing (Graham and Perin 2007; National Council of Teachers of English 2008; National Writing Project and Nagin 2006). Using digital writing tools helps them organize their ideas, keep track of their sources, share drafts, collaborate with peers, and publish to a worldwide audience.

4. What about plagiarism?

While a number of students will always choose to steal work, most students I encounter are working hard to develop their own ideas and enter the academic conversation. Scaffolding students throughout the writing process, especially in conferences, is the best way to make sure they are producing their own work, but even that is not always possible. In any case, I am a strong advocate *against* using plagiarism-detection software—it immediately puts students in a defensive position and is likely to harm relationships we have worked hard to build. Creating unique assignments, helping students develop their own approach to the topic, discussing the reasons for citing sources (Gilmore 2008; Thomas and Sassi 2011), and using digital tools such as Easy Bib, Citelighter, or Zotero is our best defense against plagiarism. Refer to Appendix A for some thoughtful ways to construct writing assignments, as well as to add a digital twist.

5. What about access? What happens when our students don't have regular opportunities to use these tools?

Despite Milton Chen's optimistic insistence that "one-to-one access is now the digital civil right of every student to fully participate in his or her own education" (Chen 2010) and the many recent calls for "anytime, anyplace" learning, it is clear that universal access remains a dream in many homes, let alone in our classrooms. The sad reality in our country is that not everyone has access to the new technologies, or the bandwidth to use the Internet effectively.

The best way for me to answer this question is by saying that we need to be our own advocates, as well as advocates for students. As millions of smart phones and tablets hit the market, many individuals, businesses, and more fortunate schools will be augmenting or replacing their computer inventories. I strongly encourage educators to work with local funding agencies and other stakeholders to identify likely sources of gently used equipment that can be returned to productive use in student hands. While I do not have personal experience with the organization, InterConnection.org is one such group.

Nearly all mobile devices can access the Internet via Wi-Fi. Finding free Wi-Fi access—through the local library or other openly available networks—is one way for students to get connected. Design assignments that don't need to be finished in class, but instead could welcome students to use the power of their network—both people and technology—over time. Many websites and apps help you locate free and open Wi-Fi networks, and many provide online tools that allow students to make audio and video recordings and enter text on mobile devices.

While the answers I have provided to these FAQs are brief, my hope is that they give you ways to begin conversations with colleagues, parents, administrators, and colleagues about how and why digital writing matters, and needs to be taught explicitly to our students. We now turn our attention to one student's digital writing, and ask questions to think about what she has learned in the process.

Exploring Craft: Looking Closely at One Student's Digital Writing

A National Writing Project colleague, Kevin Hodgson, offers his sixth graders various opportunities to craft digital writing, many of which he documents on his blog, http://dogtrax.edublogs.org. When I asked whether he would be willing to share some examples of student work, he immediately replied with links to Lydia Touchette's collection of digital writing, which include a comic strip, a video game, short essays, book reviews, podcasts, Glogster posters, and a digital story. Also, because I wanted to look at them with fresh eyes and use Lydia's work to prompt my own thinking, I did not accept Kevin's generous offer to annotate these examples with his goals for the assignment or his assessment of her work. Thus, rather than present a detailed craft analysis for each piece, as I've done in previous chapters, I'll use a "habits of mind" lens to think through what it is writers *do* in the process of crafting digital writing, as well as raise questions about what Lydia has accomplished (and what Hodgson may have been aiming for with the assignment).

Before proceeding, I encourage you to go online and read, view, and listen to each of Lydia's pieces. You may also want to familiarize yourself with some of the protocols for looking at student work, available at http://www.lasw.org or in the second edition of Blythe, Allen, and Powell's *Looking Together at Student Work* (2007) and explore Appendix A, "Creating a Digital Writing Assignment." The protocols will help you and your colleagues frame productive conversations around students' work, which is essentially what I am modeling in my comments on Lydia's work below. Also, I again mention Appendix A because the ways in which we develop assignments and ask students to enter the writing process matter a great deal. As you look at Lydia's work, I encourage you to think about why and how Hodgson designed the assignments the way that he did. Even though you can't see any specific prompts here from him, what do you imagine his goals as a teacher of digital writing might be?

Example One: Comic Strip

In this comic, a child asks her grandmother about cyberbullying, followed by two frames in which one youth replies to another after being bullied online. In the concluding frame the grandmother says that cyberbullying "is not nice." The grand-

Figure 8.1

daughter character who asks the question appears to be someone who might be susceptible to bullying because of her appearance.

Even though the child has asked only what cyberbullying is, and the grandmother just describes how it takes place, I'm struck by the way Lydia includes "details and examples" by showing two characters, each in their own bedroom, interacting online, one of them taking some agency by standing up to the cyber-bully. The implication is that we have agency in the ways we react to others.

Questions this example raises include:

- *Engagement*—The title of the comic is "No Cyberbullying!" Given the current discussions in our schools and legislatures, how does Lydia's choice of title, as well as the comic-strip genre/medium, make a connection with her audience?

- *Persistence*—Was this a single assignment done in a short time, perhaps a single class period in the computer lab, or the culminating activity for a specific set of lessons on Internet safety? Did students have a choice about the media to use?

- *Creativity*
  - Why has Lydia positioned the child and the grandmother within the frames as she has?
  - Oftentimes, comic strips have little boxes that say *Meanwhile* or something of that sort to indicate a change of location or plot from panel to panel. How might that have made Lydia's example clearer?
  - What additional elements would develop the characters? Might the granddaughter admit to having been cyberbullied and thus provide an overarching story?

- Now, imagine that you were designing an assignment that would elicit this type of digital writing. With this comic and the other work in this chapter, frame the MAPS, and think about how to invite students into this piece of writing:
  - *Mode:* _____
  - *Media:* _____
  - *Audience:* _____
  - *Purpose:* _____
  - *Situation:* _____

Example Two: Three Screenshots from **Earth and Its Layers** *Video Game Made with* **Gamestar Mechanic**

This first screen shot is the game's opening panel. The gamer is asked, "Are you ready and prepared?" and told that the goals and rules are to "stay alive while traveling through the earth." I assume the game was created during a unit on geology when Lydia was studying scientific concepts such as the mantle and crust of the Earth.

Gamestar Mechanic First Screen

Figure 8.2

Figure 8.3

The second screen shows a specific level (the second of six), "Upper Mantle." The description reads, "The Upper Mantle is the 2 layer of Earth. Together the crust and upper mantle make up the lithosphere," and the gamer is instructed to "Reach the Goal Block."

In the third screen the gamer's avatar is in the bottom-left corner, ready to move down the path toward the goal. There are a number of treasure chests, gift boxes, stars, items that look like gears, and enemy-like creatures on the screen.

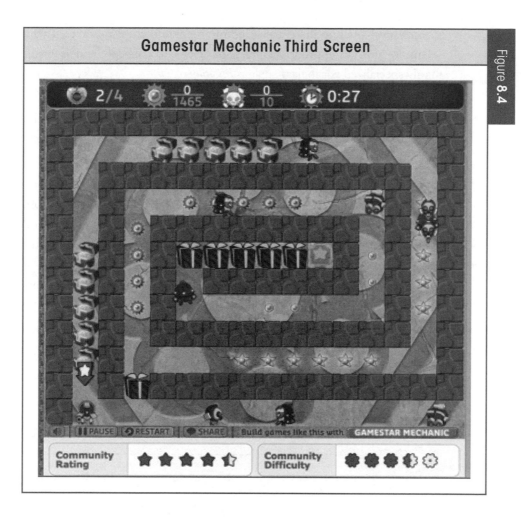

Figure 8.4

Questions this digital writing raises include:

- *Curiosity*—Before beginning to design the game, what did Lydia know about the geology of the earth? What knowledge made her able to construct each level of the game, moving from the earth's crust to its core?

- *Metacognition*—What other kinds of writing did Lydia do while creating the game? Did she create storyboards or draft the introductions to the levels? What type of writing and reading brought Lydia to the point that she was able to create the descriptions for the different levels?

- *Responsibility*—While there are some minor grammatical mistakes, Lydia seems to have an appropriate grasp of scientific concepts and is using highly specialized vocabulary such as *lithosphere*.

- *Openness*—This piece can be considered informational and narrative—creative nonfiction of sorts. In what ways has Lydia positioned you, the gamer, as both a reader and as an interactive participant? What else might you need to learn or be able to do in order to fully understand the definitions and concepts she is presenting?

- *Flexibility*—Many scholars who advocate using video games in education, most notably James Paul Gee (2003), have described the ways playing and creating games can be highly engaging, helping students become better problem solvers and creative thinkers. How did Kevin introduce some of the ideas about game theory to his students, and how do those ideas show up in the design of Lydia's game?

- Again, think about the assignment itself, and frame the MAPS for this piece of writing:

  - *Mode:* _____

  - *Media:* _____

  - *Audience:* _____

  - *Purpose:* _____

  - *Situation:* _____

Example Three: **The Westing Game *Book Review/Blog Post***

In this brief review, Lydia summarizes key elements of the book (setting, names of the characters, and the main conflict) and poses questions for the reader. The image of the book cover appears to be cited from another blog post. Lydia did not use any tags to categorize her post. Perhaps most important, at least most interesting, this review was posted at 6:15 PM, a time outside the school day.

Questions this piece of digital writing raises iniclude:

- *Creativity*—Is this a typical book review for Kevin's students in terms of length and detail? Does he ask students to post brief reviews of the books they read individually on a class blog so that the other students

---

Blog Post

The Westing Game

leave a comment _____

http://3.bp.blogspot.com/-STOvXZLOD58/Ty1QHI-c7AI/AAAAAAAADUg/dMVeOA5sKK0/s1600/Cover.jpg

I read the book, The Westing Game. It is a very well written book that has been adapted into a movie. Sixteen individuals are chosen in queer ways to live in Sunset Towers. They are called together to hear the will of Samuel W. Westing which is in the form of a puzzle. The sixteen individuals are divided into 8 groups to try and solve the riddle. Who will be the first to figure it out? Will it be Turtle and Baba or Judge Ford and Mr. McSouthers? Or Theo and Doug or Grace and Mr. Hoo ? Or will it be another group or will it NEVER be solved ????

Written by norrisbooks | Posted in Uncategorized
May 15, 2012 at 6:15 pm

---

can see them, essentially replacing the "book talk" so many of us are familiar with?

- *Engagement*—Has Lydia read other book reviews, perhaps on sites like Amazon.com or GoodReads, as examples? Since this is a web-based text, might she have included links to other reviewers who found the book entertaining (or didn't like it), the author's website, or the movie trailer?

- Comparing this to a more traditional book report, frame the MAPS for this piece of writing:
  - *Mode:* _____
  - *Media:* _____
  - *Audience:* _____
  - *Purpose:* _____
  - *Situation:* _____

Example Four: "Nuclear Power" Glogster Poster, Essay, and Word Cloud

In these three components of a project on nuclear power, Lydia shares what she has learned about the topic using three separate media.

In the poster, Lydia embeds clip art of an atom, two YouTube videos, and an aerial photograph of a nuclear power plant. In terms of the Robin Williams' CRAP principles—contrast, repetition, alignment, and proximity—her poster is broken up into seven distinct segments: the title takes up the top, and an imaginary table, two columns with three rows, balances the images with facts about nuclear power. (The position of the images and the statements alternate.) Two items seem to be informational (the text box about Fermi and the picture of the power plant); the other four lean more toward making an argument about nuclear power. While Lydia does not specifically state her position on whether we should use nuclear power, she gives her opinion about where nuclear plants should be located. Since the Common Core State Standards expect a transition from opinion to argument writing in sixth grade, the poster could trigger a writing conference about those genres.

The essay follows a traditional format in which Lydia compares and contrasts the benefits and downfalls of nuclear power, citing two Internet sources. She ends with a firmer stand on the benefits side of the issue but offers a number of safety considerations: protection of human and animal life, location of power plants in relation to earthquake zones, and storage of the spent nuclear fuel. In the last paragraph, she states: "As this is the way of the future we should try to fix the kinks now so that when we really need nuclear power it will be ready." By acknowledging both sides of the issue, she is practicing the skill of rebuttal, which will become more and more a part of her argumentative writing as she moves through middle and high school.

In the word cloud Lydia applies visual display elements to many of the words from her essay. Without knowing the extent to which Lydia was able to manipulate the size, color, orientation, and placement of the words in this cloud (they are advanced features in the software), I can't say for sure that she's done this as intentionally as I hope she has. Nevertheless, a few unique aspects are worth noting. First, the colors she chose are part of a dark, earth-toned palette. Given her concern about the effects of nuclear power on the planet, this seems apt. Second, the triangular placement of the three biggest words—*power*, *nuclear*, and *people*—both connect them and establish a tension among them. Finally, she did not include common words such as *a* or *the*.

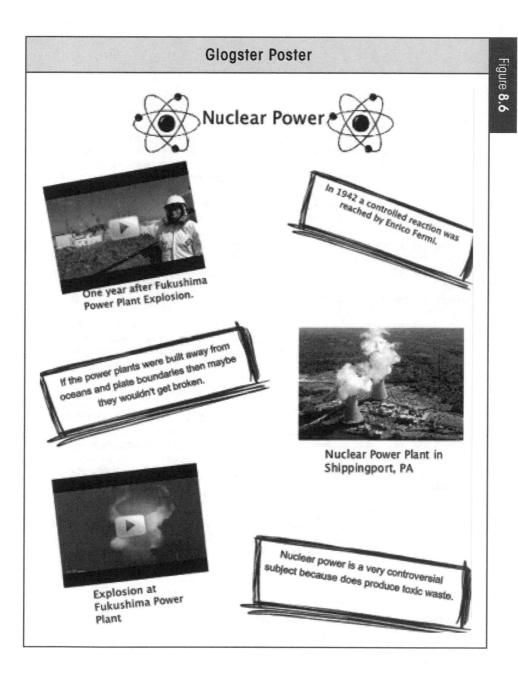

Figure **8.6**

Figure 8.7

Essay

NUCLEAR POWER   Lydia Touchette

On March 11, 2011 the Fukushima Power Plant in Japan was disabled by a tsunami. The water walls had not stopped the tsunami because the earthquake had shifted the ground. All three of the reactors melted and began to release radiation. Nuclear power plants have been around for about 70 years. It provides an alternate power source other than oil or coal. Many people have people have opposing ideas about it.

Even thousands of years ago the search for an alternate power source was on. In 100 BC a Greek philosopher invented the piston that led to the first successful steam engine in 1712. In 1823 Jacob Perkins produced super heated steam and the first practical combustion engine was made in 1860. These were the inventions that led to the nuclear power plants of today. In 1942 Enrico Fermi reached a controlled nuclear chain reaction.[1] In 1957 a functional nuclear power plant began operation in Shippingport, Pennsylvania.[2] From there we have produced atomic bombs and nuclear power plants that may not have been for the best.

Nuclear power can be a good thing if it is protected and radiation is not released. If there was not the chance of radiation being released if there was an accident, then I would be totally for it. Yet because there is and people and animals are hurt by it, it is a very controversial idea. Many people support the idea that nuclear power is dangerous energy and that it should be stopped. People say that the waste from the power plants is too much. But other people say that it the way of the future and we should go for it.

The world should try to come up with ideas that don't produce waste. It would help our world highly. The power plants could also be built in places where they can't be hit with tsunamis. Although no place is completely safe from earthquakes, the plants could be built away from plate boundaries so that they can't be broken. As for the waste people say you could dispose of it on the sun or in space. You can also dry store it and wet store it.

I really believe that people can make a change if they just try. Nuclear power could be good if the people of the world tried to make a difference. As this is the way of the future we should try to fix the kinks now so that when we really need nuclear power it will be ready. Nuclear Power will some day keep our world safe. Nuclear Power is a great alternative to oil or coal.

References:

1. http://library.thinkquest.org/17658/nuc/nuchistoryht.html\

2.Custodio, Theresa. "Nuclear Power Plants in the U.S." *EHow*. Demand Media, 05 Mar. 2011. Web. 05 June 2012. <http://www.ehow.com/info_8030064_nuclear-power-plants.html>.

Figure 8.8

Word Cloud Using Wordle.net

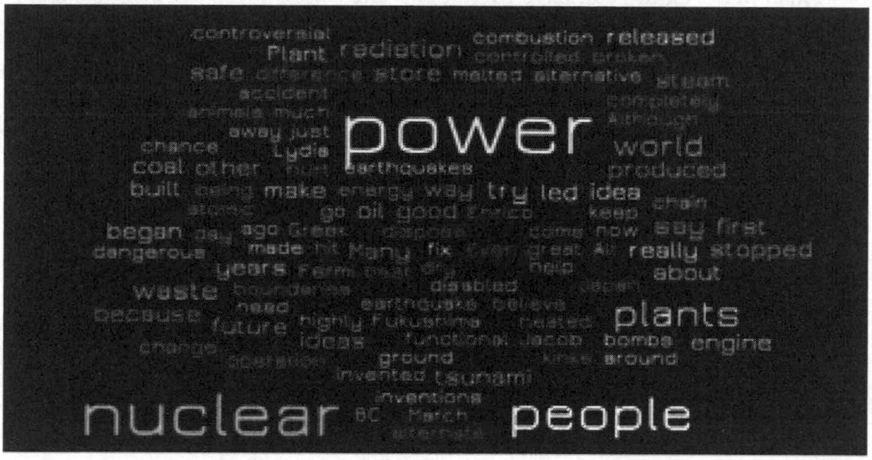

Questions these pieces of digital writing raise include:

- *Persistence*—Clearly, this was not a one-day assignment. How did Kevin support his students throughout the research process? How did Lydia choose nuclear power as her topic? Were students given specific directions about what to include in the poster, essay, and word cloud?

- *Creativity*—As Lydia designed the graphic texts, to what degree was she consciously making the argument in her essay evident? To the extent that these texts blend informational and argumentative writing, how did Lydia make choices about what examples would be most useful in the visuals (the Fukushima videos, the words *power*, *nuclear*, *people*)?

- *Curiosity*—How might she have used the visuals, especially the poster, to present pro/con information? Might it have made sense to include one text, one image, and one video element on each side of the issue?

- *Openness*—Could Lydia have recorded herself reading her essay and put a brief video clip into the Glogster?

■ *Responsibility*—In the Wordle word cloud, what other words may have been necessary? What words were really unnecessary (*BC*, *Enrico*, and *March*, for instance)? Could she have included some other terms about nuclear power or references to nuclear power accidents such as Chernobyl or Three Mile Island?

■ Considering the collection of pieces present here, frame the MAPS for this multigenre project:

● *Modes:* _____

● *Media:* _____

● *Audience:* _____

● *Purpose:* _____

● *Situation:* _____

Scan to listen
to podcast.

Example Five: Lego Harry Potter Years 1–4 *Game Review Podcast*

Scan here to listen to Lydia's podcast or visit http://goo.gl/wZMsB. A transcript is provided below.

I reviewed the game, *Lego Harry Potter Years 1–4.* The game is based on the Harry Potter books, 1–4. It is played on the Nintendo DS. The player uses the arrow and the A, B, Y, and X buttons and the pen to find hidden gems and hats to help you buy things and to learn spells and to meet and defeat people, trolls, and monsters.

　The background music is the theme song from Harry Potter. It is perfect for the game. The graphics are okay. They use Lego people, but probably could have done better if used animated characters. The game is perfectly balanced between challenging and impossible. It can seem impossible if you haven't played before, but gets easier as you go on. For just a few dollars, you can explore the *magical* story of Harry Potter.

This is a concise review. Lydia mentions a number of generic features of the game, including the graphic interface, the adventure, the villains, and the level of challenge. She could have included more specific examples about the characters that the gamer gets to play such as Harry, Ron, and Hermione. She might also have described some of the specific scenes in the game and how they align with scenes from the books. She makes an interesting financial appeal at the end: "For just a few dollars. . . ."

Questions this piece of digital writing raises include:

- *Flexibility*—In what ways is a review composed specifically to be audio-recorded different from a printed review? How is a review of a game (essentially a narrative in which the gamer takes part) similar to and different from a review of a book or movie (in which the reader or viewer has no control over the action)?

- *Responsibility*—How does Lydia's tone and cadence in the podcast affect your impression of her as a reviewer? Do you think she enjoyed the game? How does her emphasis on the word *magical* work for you as a listener?

- *Creativity*—Given the ambient noise in the background, what situational constraints do you think Lydia faced in recording this audio text (time, location, equipment)? How might Lydia have overcome those constraints or at least used them to her advantage?

- As an audio text, frame the MAPS for this piece of writing:
  - *Mode:* _____
  - *Media:* _____
  - *Audience:* _____
  - *Purpose:* _____
  - *Situation:* _____

Final Thoughts on Lydia's Work

Reflecting on Lydia's work, I recognize that there are areas for improvement, as we would expect with any sixth grader. However, as someone who has carefully crafted digital writing, she certainly demonstrates the many skills that Lucy Spence (2009) outlines.

> *Multiple literacy practices include traditional literacies such as English reading and writing but also include using additional verbal languages,*

computer-related discourse, Internet searches, and skill in handling de-
vices such as the mouse, keyboard, scanner, and printer. Literacy practices
extend over a broad range of communicative modes in today's world, in-
cluding dance, music, drawing, video, and audio technology. (595)

Lydia has invited us into a rich array of literate practices, and I hope you have begun to think more deeply about the possibilities in crafting digital writing. While you may not yet be ready to have your students use all these media, you should be able to see the value in Lydia's thinking and what she has accomplished as a thoughtful, literate young adult. Also, my hope is that you have a better sense of how you can design digital writing assignments using a variety of topics, genres, and digital writing tools.

Bringing It Together: A Senior Exit Portfolio

Scan to view portfolio.

Although I risk being accused of nepotism, I'll be a proud dad and share the senior exit portfolio of someone I know quite well: my son, Tyler (https://sites.google .com/site/tylerdavidhicks). When he discovered he would be required to create a digital portfolio, he was a bit daunted by the prospect of putting together a website. Students in previous years had produced tangible binders and folders of texts and artifacts using them as the basis for a thirty-minute presentation to a panel comprising the English teacher, another teacher from the school, and a community member. Creating a website was something even this digital native wasn't accustomed to doing, and it presented a challenge for him.

During one trimester of the senior year, Tyler's English teacher taught the class how to use Google Sites to share the artifacts and reflections required by the relevant academic and career and college readiness standards. Once Tyler was able to create a basic organizational structure for his portfolio, he began tagging and organizing the component artifacts. He did have trouble getting everything scanned and converted into PDF files, but ultimately succeeded. Realizing that he would have had to compile a physical portfolio from a mess of papers on his bedroom floor, he said, "The digital portfolio made me be more creative, because it was more pragmatic and efficient." One of the main reasons his teacher required a digital portfolio was efficiency, and I can't blame her. Carrying dozens of senior exit portfolios home and going through them is an arduous task.

Tyler's Portfolio Homepage

Figure 8.9

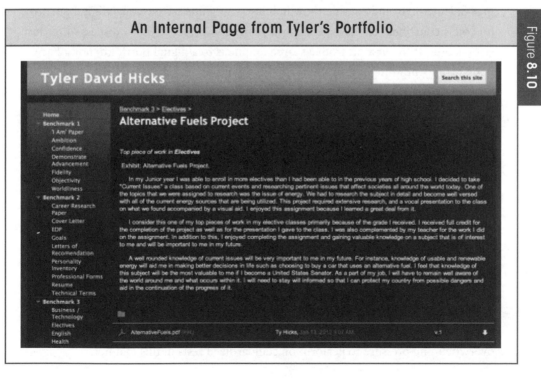

An Internal Page from Tyler's Portfolio

Figure 8.10

During his panel presentation, Tyler was able to click on individual artifacts as the panel asked him questions. While he did have prepared remarks, the portfolio's digital format allowed him to be more flexible.

> *The [portfolio] program caused me to reflect on the things I had done in high school and find some value in them. The digital tools gave me more room to be creative. They gave me more time to make my portfolio worth looking at. Being able to keep it organized was nice. It enabled me to keep drafts and revise. (Personal interview)*

Still, even though Tyler had not handwritten a formal paper for school since his late elementary years and was quite adept at using technology, he struggled at first, conceptually and practically. He needed a teacher—as well as weekly mini-lessons and an overall rubric and checklist—to guide him. This intentional, scaffolded set of procedures helped him tie everything together and represent himself to his best advantage. I invite you to take a look at what he accomplished (see Figures 8.9 and 8.10) and consider how helping your students develop a digital portfolio could contribute to the type of positive, online presence that I discussed in the last chapter. If the first hit from a search engine is to a digital portfolio, not a Facebook profile, how might that affect the ways that our digital writers see themselves?

Charting Your Next Steps Toward Teaching Digital Writing

My hope for you, as you move forward in your quest to teach the craft of digital writing, is that this book is merely a starting point. Using the examples in this text and the many more you and your students will create, you can continue the conversation about crafting digital writing in your classroom, school, and community.

Mark Warschauer (2011), who has a long and respected history of studying technology implementation in schools, responds to today's core standards and the overwhelming pressure to perform on standardized tests in this manner.

> *When the predominant assessments we have in many schools are multiple-choice tests, there's little incentive to incorporate powerful digital media in instruction, since the value of [these] media is to promote more authentic forms of learning that are not yet tested. However, the more we seek to assess students' ability to write meaningful papers, conduct authentic research, analyze scientific data, and solve ill-structured problems, the more value [these] digital media will have to instruction.* (83–84)

I agree. We are not "giving up" traditional academic literacies by asking students to craft digital writing. We are actually asking them to do more.

But I want to push the conversation about digital writing even further. We can and should ask students to do what Ken Robinson calls "deliberate" work. We need to ask our digital writers to work with intention. This requires that we keep thinking, taking risks, learning from our mistakes, and working each day to model and mentor them in the craft of digital writing. Given the many examples in this book—as well as the countless ones you can find and create with your own students—my hope is that you are ready to teach your writers about the craft of digital writing. And, I hope that you share what you have found with others, be it by blogging, tweeting, or sharing on the book's wiki page: http://digitalwritingworkshop .wikispaces.com/Crafting_Digital_Writing

Thanks for all that you do, and I look forward to continuing our conversation.

APPENDIX A: CREATING A DIGITAL WRITING ASSIGNMENT

n addition to the MAPS heuristic that I have used throughout the book, I want to recommend two of other sources for creating writing assignments and then add a digital twist.

First, I point to Traci Gardner's aptly titled *Designing Writing Assignments* (Gardner 2008). Here, she succinctly describes the three actions that go into successful writing assignments: "Define the writing task," "Explore the expectations," "Provide supporting materials and activities" (35). She elaborates on each of these ideas, suggesting that teachers work with students to clarify each of these components depending on the context of the writing assignment, especially in relation to the genre. In a subsequent chapter, she suggests alternative points of view, positions, time frames, sources for research, and a comprehensive list of genres using the heuristic of RAFTS (Role, Audience, Format, Topic, and Strong Verb). While Gardner does mention a few digital writing types such as blogs and websites, I would suggest that you could take most of the genres she lists and turn them into digital texts.

For instance, she suggests postcards as one genre. What might a "digital postcard" look like? Students may first think of e-cards, yet then could broaden their horizons to think about creating a blog with pictures of postcards that they create. Or, perhaps they could design an online poster or photo collage with many of the typical slogans, fonts, and styles of postcards. Perhaps they could find archival images of postcards and use a photo-editing program to insert newer images of the place. No matter what the writing context, Gardner's many suggestions can be enhanced with the endless application of digital tools. A historical narrative with hyperlinks to primary sources? A set of government statistics reimagined as an infographic? A sonnet transformed into a word cloud? The possibilities for digital writing are endless.

Second, I encourage you to look at the National Writing Project's *Writing Assignment Framework and Overview* (National Writing Project 2011), which offers teachers "a lens to look at an assignment's purpose, planning preparation, expectations, and processes." In addition to the very smart questions that this document asks us to consider as teachers of writing, I would add a few more for digital writing.

- Who are the audiences, intended and incidental, who might encounter this piece of digital writing?

- How could the assignment invite students to use digital writing tools to identify, organize, and extend their ideas?

- Is the writing assignment designed to be digitally convenient (available for easy access online) or digitally enhanced (taking advantage of multimedia components)?

- To what extent do students have choice over the technologies they will use to create this piece of digital writing?

- Does the assignment ask students to create original media, remix existing media, or do some combination of both?

- In what ways is the student invited to reflect on his or her own work through the use of digital tools such as screencasting or commenting features?

- If a collaborative project, how will writing tasks be divided so individual students are contributing equal amounts of thinking toward the content and design of the digital text?

Both Gardner's book and the NWP Framework offer us smart ways for designing effective writing assignments, and some simple adaptations could also turn them into digital writing assignments, too.

APPENDIX B: WHAT'S NEW, WHAT'S NEXT: WEBSITES AND APPS

A common question that I am asked during professional development workshops or courses that I teach boils down to this: How do you keep up with all the possible technologies that are available? Answering honestly, I say simply: "I can't." In working with colleagues through my role as director of the Chippewa River Project at Central Michigan University, within the broader professional communities of the National Writing Project and the National Council of Teachers of English, and through various roles as a conference presenter and consultants, I am constantly learning about what's new and what's next. I often joke that if it looks like I am staying one step ahead of you, that is only because I learned something new *this morning* and not because I'm any smarter.

Another strategy that I used to stay current on the latest in edtech is to subscribe to a variety of blogs through Google Reader and I follow Twitter feeds of many teacher leaders. Using an app called Flipboard (http://flipboard.com/), I am able to read the latest blog posts and tweets in an appealing, magazine-style format. If I find something interesting, I can quickly email myself a link to the article. This has become a major form of professional reading for me, although I also read books, journals, the *NCTE Inbox* Newsletter, NCLE SmartBrief, eSchool News, Edutopia, and the blog of Richard Byrne: www.freetech4teachers.com.

Finally, the crowd-sourced website alternativeTo.net (http://alternativeto.net) offers an ever-growing list of "alternatives to software you already know and want to replace," whether for practical reasons—your software is getting old—or because you want to join in the free and open source movement. Either way, alternativeTo.net is a vibrant community of users who will help you make decisions about which software, websites, and mobile apps make the most sense for you.

No sooner will this book go to print than the resources list will need to be updated. A website will suddenly disappear, a new one will come on the scene, and we will move on to teaching writing the best way that we know how. One lesson that I learned after making a companion website for my first book was that websites can disappear, or at least become cost prohibitive, very quickly.

I will attempt, with your help, to maintain a list of websites and apps for digital writing at: http://digitalwritingworkshop.wikispaces.com/Websites_And_Apps. Please visit the website and go from there.

Please join the wiki so we can all share and learn together.

Scan to view resources for *Crafting Digital Writing.*

APPENDIX C

Studying a Piece of Digital Writing: What Do You Notice?

Title of Piece: _____

Mode (Genre): _____

Audience/Purpose: _____

Situation/Context: _____

Text/Speech/Writing	Photos/Video

How do these elements work together to create an overall effect?

Narration/Music/Sound Effects	Other Media/Transitions/Effects

Concept map adapted from Franki Sibberson, "Mentor Texts in the Digital Writing Owrkshop" Presentation, 2011. Used with permission.

REFERENCES

Anderson, J. 2011. *Ten Things Every Writer Needs to Know*. Stenhouse Publishers.

Atwell, N. 1998. *In the Middle: New Understandings About Writing, Reading, and Learning* (2nd ed.). Portsmouth, NH: Boynton/Cook.

———. 2002. *Lessons That Change Writers*. Portsmouth, NH: Firsthand/Heinemann.

Bass, W. 2012a, January 9. Mentor Text in the Digital Writing Workshop: Cultural Participation. Retrieved from http://blog.mrbassonline.com/2012/01/mentor-text-in-the-digital-writing-workshop-cultural-participation/.

———. 2012b, January 10. Mentoring Technique. Retrieved from http://blog.mrbassonline.com/2012/01/mentoring-technique/.

———. 2012c, January 11. Mentoring a Process. Retrieved from http://blog.mrbassonline.com/2012/01/mentoring-a-process/.

Bauerlein, M. 2008. *The Dumbest Generation: How the Digital Age Stupefies Young Americans and Jeopardizes Our Future* (1st ed.). New York: Tarcher.

Beach, R. 2006. *Teachingmedialiteracy.com: A Web-Linked Guide to Resources and Activities*. New York: Teachers College Press.

Beach, R., C. Anson, L.-A. K. Breuch, and T. Swiss. 2008. *Teaching Writing Using Blogs, Wikis, and Other Digital Tools*. Norwood, MA: Christopher-Gordon Publishers, Inc.

Beach, R., A. H. Thein, and A. Webb. 2012. *Teaching to Exceed the English Language Arts Common Core State Standards: A Literacy Practices Approach for 6–12 Classrooms*. New York: Routledge.

Blythe, T., D. Allen, and B. S. Powell. 2007. *Looking Together at Student Work* (2nd ed.). New York: Teachers College Press.

BrainyQuote. n.d.. Ira Glass Quotes. Retrieved August 15, 2012, from http://www.brainyquote.com/quotes/authors/i/ira_glass.html.

Brockman, E., M. Taylor, M. Kreth, and M. K. Crawford. 2011. What Do Professors Really Say About College Writing? *English Journal*, *100*(3), 75–81.

Burke, J. 2011, February 22. The Digital Essay—English Companion Ning. Retrieved August 13, 2012, from http://englishcompanion.ning.com/forum/topics/the-digital-essay.

Bush, J., and L. A. Zuidema. 2011. Beyond Language: The Grammar of Document Design. *English Journal*, *100*(4), 86–89.

Calkins, L. M. 1994. *The Art of Teaching Writing*. Portsmouth, NH: Heinemann.

Calkins, L., M. Ehrenworth, and C. Lehman. 2012. *Pathways to the Common Core: Accelerating Achievement*. Portsmouth, NH: Heinemann.

Calkins, L., A. Hartman, and Z. R. White. 2005. *One to One: The Art of Conferring with Young Writers*. Portsmouth, NH: Heinemann.

Carr, N. 2010. *The Shallows: What the Internet Is Doing to Our Brains* (1st ed.). New York: W. W. Norton & Company.

Chase, Z., and D. Laufenberg. 2011. Embracing the Squishiness of Digital Literacy. *Journal of Adolescent & Adult Literacy 54*(7), 535–537.

Chen, M. 2010. *Education Nation: Six Leading Edges of Innovation in Our Schools*. San Francisco: John Wiley and Sons.

Coiro, J. 2011. Talking About Reading as Thinking: Modeling the Hidden Complexities of Online Reading Comprehension. *Theory Into Practice, 50*(2), 107–115. doi:10.1080/00405841.2011.558435.

Colfer, E. 2009. *Artemis Fowl: The Lost Colony* (Reprint). New York: Hyperion Book CH.

Common Core State Standards Initiative. 2010. Common Core State Standards Initiative | The Standards | English Language Arts Standards. Retrieved April 5, 2011, from www.corestandards.org/the-standards/english-language-arts-standards.

Consortium for School Networking. 2011, September 13. Acceptable Use Policies in the Web 2.0 and Mobile Era. Retrieved August 18, 2012, from www.cosn.org/Initiatives/ParticipatoryLearning/Web20MobileAUPGuide/tabid/8139/Default.aspx

Council of Writing Program Administrators, National Council of Teachers of English, and National Writing Project. 2011, January. *Framework for Success in Postsecondary Writing* | Council of Writing Program Administrators. Retrieved August 12, 2012, from http://wpacouncil.org/framework

Davidson, C. N. 2011. *Now You See It: How the Brain Science of Attention Will Transform the Way We Live, Work, and Learn* (1st ed.). New York: Viking Penguin.

Dean, D. 2008. *Genre Theory: Teaching, Writing, and Being*. Urbana, IL: National Council of Teachers of English.

Dorfman, L. R., and R. Cappelli. 2007. *Mentor Texts: Teaching Writing Through Children's Literature, K–6*. Portland, ME: Stenhouse Publishers.

———. 2009. *Nonfiction Mentor Texts: Teaching Informational Writing Through Children's Literature, K–8*. Portland, ME: Stenhouse Publishers.

Duarte, N. 2008. *slide:ology: The Art and Science of Creating Great Presentations* (1st ed.). Sebastopol, CA: O'Reilly Media.

Duke, N. K., S. Caughplan, M. Juzwik, and N. Martin. 2011. *Reading and Writing Genre with Purpose in K–8 Classrooms*. Portsmouth, NH: Heinemann.

Ewald, W., K. Hyde, and L. Lord. 2011. *Literacy and Justice Through Photography: A Classroom Guide*. New York: Teachers College Press.

Flanders, V. n. d.. Top 30 Web Design Mistakes. Retrieved August 18, 2012, from www.webpagesthatsuck.com/top-30-web-design-mistakes.html.

Fleischer, C., and S. Andrew-Vaughan. 2009. *Writing Outside Your Comfort Zone: Helping Students Navigate Unfamiliar Genres*. Portsmouth, NH: Heinemann.

Fletcher, R. 1992. *What a Writer Needs*. Portsmouth, NH: Heinemann.

———. 2010. *Pyrotechnics on the Page: Playful Craft That Sparks Writing*. Portland, ME: Stenhouse Publishers.

———. 2011. *Mentor Author, Mentor Texts: Short Texts, Craft Notes, and Practical Classroom Uses*. Portsmouth, NH: Heinemann.

Fletcher, R., and J. Portalupi. 1998. *Craft Lessons: Teaching Writing K-8*. Portland, ME: Stenhouse Publishers.

———. 2001. *Writing Workshop: The Essential Guide*. Portsmouth, NH: Heinemann.

Fountas, I., and G. S. Pinnell. 2012. *Genre Study: Teaching with Fiction and Nonfiction Books*. Portsmouth, NH: Heinemann.

Fredricksen, J. E., J. D. Wilhelm, and M. Smith. 2012. *So, What's the Story?: Teaching Narrative to Understand Ourselves, Others, and the World*. Portsmouth, NH: Heinemann.

Gallagher, K. 2011. *Write Like This: Teaching Real-World Writing Through Modeling and Mentor Texts*. Portland, ME: Stenhouse Publishers.

———. 2012, August 14. Kelly Gallagher—Resources. Retrieved August 15, 2012, from http://kellygallagher.org/resources/articles.html.

Gardner, T. 2008. *Designing Writing Assignments*. Urbana, IL: National Council of Teachers of English.

Gee, J. P. 2003. *What Video Games Have to Teach Us About Literacy and Learning*. New York: Palgrave McMillan.

Gilmore, B. 2008. *Plagiarism: Why It Happens and How to Prevent It*. Portsmouth, NH: Heinemann.

Gladwell, M. 2002. *The Tipping Point: How Little Things Can Make a Big Difference* (Reprint ed.). Boston: Back Bay Books.

Godin, S. 2012. *Stop Stealing Dreams (What Is School For?)*. Retrieved from www.sethgodin.com/sg/docs/stopstealingdreamsscreen.pdf.

Golden, J. 2001. *Reading in the Dark: Using Film as a Tool in the English Classroom*. New York: National Council of Teachers of English.

———. 2006. *Reading in the Reel World: Teaching Documentaries and Other Nonfiction Texts*. New York: National Council of Teachers of English.

Graff, G., C. Birkenstein, and R. Durst. 2011. *They Say, I Say: The Moves That Matter in Academic Writing with Readings* (Second ed.). New York: W. W. Norton & Company.

Graham, S., and D. Perin. 2007. *Writing Next: Effective Strategies to Improve Writing of Adolescents in Middle and High Schools*. Washington, DC: Alliance for Excellent Education. Retrieved from www.all4ed.org/files/WritingNext.pdf.

Graves, D. H., and P. Kittle. 2005. *Inside Writing: How to Teach the Details of Craft*. Portsmouth, NH: Heinemann.

Hale, E. 2008. *Crafting Writers, K–6*. Portland, ME: Stenhouse Publishers.

Heath, C., and D. Heath. 2007. *Made to Stick: Why Some Ideas Survive and Others Die* (1st ed.). New York: Random House.

Herrington, A., K. Hodgson, and C. Moran. 2009. *Teaching the New Writing: Technology, Change, and Assessment in the 21st-Century Classroom*. New York: Teachers College Press.

Hicks, T. 2009. *The Digital Writing Workshop*. Portsmouth, NH: Heinemann.

Hicks, T., C. A. Young, S. B. Kajder, and B. Hunt. 2012. Same as It Ever Was: Enacting the Promise of Teaching, Writing, and New Media. *English Journal*, *101*(3), 68–74.

Hillocks, G. Jr. 2006. *Narrative Writing: Learning a New Model for Teaching*. Portsmouth, NH: Heinemann.

———. 2011. *Teaching Argument Writing, Grades 6–12: Supporting Claims with Relevant Evidence and Clear Reasoning*. Portsmouth, NH: Heinemann.

Hobbs, R. 2010. *Copyright Clarity: How Fair Use Supports Digital Learning*. Thousand Oaks, CA: Corwin Press.

———. 2011. *Digital and Media Literacy: Connecting Culture and Classroom*. Thousand Oaks, CA: Corwin Press.

Ito, M., S. Baumer, M. Bittanti, D. Boyd, R. Cody, B. Herr-Stephenson, H. A. Horst, et al. 2009. *Hanging Out, Messing Around, and Geeking Out: Kids Living and Learning with New Media* (1st ed.). Cambridge, MA: The MIT Press.

Johnson, F. 2012. Film School for Slideware: Film, Comics, and Slideshows as Sequential Art. *Computers and Composition*, *29*(2), 124–136. doi:10.1016/j.compcom.2012.02.001.

Johnson, J. 2010a, September 3. 10 Tips for Designing Presentations That Don't Suck: Pt. 1. Retrieved from http://designshack.net/?p=11810.

———. 2010b, September 7. 10 Tips for Designing Presentations That Don't Suck: Pt. 2. Retrieved from http://designshack.net/articles/graphics/10-tips-for-designing-presentations-that-don%E2%80%99t-suck-pt-2.

Johnson, S. 2010, March 11. Guest Blog: Making the Case for Social Media in Education | Edutopia. Retrieved August 18, 2012, from www.edutopia.org/social-media-case-education-edchat-steve-johnson.

Kajder, S. 2010. *Adolescents and Digital Literacies: Learning Alongside Our Students*. Urbana, IL: National Council of Teachers of English. Retrieved from www1.ncte.org/store/books/language/130985.htm.

Kajder, S. B. 2003. *The Tech-Savvy English Classroom*. Portland, ME: Stenhouse Publishers.

———. 2004. Enter Here: Personal Narrative and Digital Storytelling. *The English Journal, 93*(3), 64–68.

Kist, W. R. 2009. *The Socially Networked Classroom: Teaching in the New Media Age*. Thousand Oaks, CA: Corwin Press.

Kittle, P. 2008. *Write Beside Them: Risk, Voice, and Clarity in High School Writing* (Pap/DVD.). Portsmouth, NH: Heinemann.

———. 2010. If Life Were a Movie, How Would You Write It? *Voices from the Middle, 17*(3), 49–50.

Lane, B. 1992. *After THE END: Teaching and Learning Creative Revision*. Portsmouth, NH: Heinemann.

———. 1999. *The Reviser's Toolbox*. Shoreham, VT: Discover Writing Press.

Lattimer, H. 2003. *Thinking Through Genre: Units of Study in Reading and Writing Workshops Grades 4–12*. Portland, ME: Stenhouse Publishers.

McLuhan, M. 2005. *Understanding Media* (2nd ed.). London: Routledge.

Miller, A. 1998. *Death of a Salesman* (1st ed.). New York: Penguin Books.

Mills, K. A. 2010. Shrek Meets Vygotsky: Rethinking Adolescents' Multimodal Literacy Practices in Schools. *Journal of Adolescent & Adult Literacy, 54*(1), 35–45. doi:10.1598/JAAL.54.1.4.

Mills, K. A., and V. Chandra. 2011. Microblogging as a Literacy Practice for Educational Communities. *Journal of Adolescent & Adult Literacy, 55*(1), 35–45. doi: 10.1598/JAAL.55.1.4.

Moline, S. 2011. *I See What You Mean: Visual Literacy K–8* (2nd ed.). Portland, ME: Stenhouse Publishers.

MSU News. 2010, September 9. LMK, IDK: Texting Is Writing, Researcher Says | MSU Research. Retrieved August 12, 2012, from http://research.msu.edu/stories/lmk-idk-texting-writing-researcher-says.

Nadel, D. 2003, November. Ten Questions for Edward Tufte. Retrieved August 13, 2012, from www.edwardtufte.com/tufte/tenquestions.

National Council of Teachers of English. 2008. Writing Now: A Policy Research Brief Produced by the National Council of Teachers of English. Retrieved December 21, 2008, from www.ncte.org/library/NCTEFiles/Resources/PolicyResearch/WrtgResearchBrief.pdf.

National Writing Project. 2011. *Writing Assignment Framework and Overview*. Retrieved from www.nwp.org/cs/public/download/nwp_file/15410/Writing_Assignment_Framework_and_Overview.pdf?x-r=pcfile_d.

National Writing Project, D. DeVoss, E. Eidman-Aadahl, and T. Hicks. 2010. *Because Digital Writing Matters: Improving Student Writing in Online and Multimedia Environments*. Hoboken, NJ: Jossey-Bass.

National Writing Project, and C. Nagin. 2006. *Because Writing Matters: Improving Student Writing in Our Schools* (Rev. Upd.). Hoboken, NJ: Jossey-Bass.

Pariser, E. 2011. *The Filter Bubble: What the Internet Is Hiding from You.* New York: Penguin Press.

Plester, B., C. Wood, and V. Bell. 2008. Txt msg n School Literacy: Does Texting and Knowledge of Text Abbreviations Adversely Affect Children's Literacy Attainment? *Literacy, 42*(3), 137–144. doi:10.1111/j.1741–4369.2008.00489.x.

Portalupi, J., and R. Fletcher. 2001. *Nonfiction Craft Lessons: Teaching Information Writing K–8.* Portland, ME: Stenhouse Publishers.

Porter, B. 2005. *DigiTales: The Art of Telling Digital Stories* (1st ed.). Denver, CO: bjpconsulting.

Postman, N. 2005. *Amusing Ourselves to Death: Public Discourse in the Age of Show Business* (Rev.). New York: Penguin Books.

Ray, K. W. 1999. *Wondrous Words: Writers and Writing in the Elementary Classroom.* Urbana, IL: National Council of Teachers of English.

———. 2010. *In Pictures and In Words: Teaching the Qualities of Good Writing Through Illustration Study* (1st ed.). Portsmouth, NH: Heinemann.

Ray, K. W., and L. Laminack. 2001. *The Writing Workshop: Working Through the Hard Parts.* Urbana, IL: National Council of Teachers of English.

Reed, D., and T. Hicks. 2009. From the Front of the Classroom to the Ears of the World: Podcasting as an Extension of Speech Class. In A. Herrington, K. Hodgson, and C. Moran (Eds.), *Teaching the New Writing: Technology, Change, and Assessment in the 21st Century Classroom* (pp. 124–139). New York: Teachers College Press/National Writing Project.

Reynolds, G. 2007, July 28. Presentation Zen: Make Your Presentations Stickier: These 3 Books Can Help. Retrieved August 13, 2012, from www .presentationzen.com/presentationzen/2007/07/make.html.

———. 2008. *Presentation Zen: Simple Ideas on Presentation Design and Delivery* (1st ed.). Berkeley, CA: New Riders Press.

Rheingold, H. 2012. *Net Smart: How to Thrive Online.* Cambridge, MA: The MIT Press.

Richardson, W. 2010. *Blogs, Wikis, Podcasts, and Other Powerful Web Tools for Classrooms* (3rd ed.). Thousand Oaks, CA: Corwin Press.

Robb, L. 2010. *Teaching Middle School Writers: What Every English Teacher Needs to Know.* Portsmouth, NH: Heinemann.

Robinson, K. 2011. *Out of Our Minds: Learning to be Creative* (2nd ed.). Chichester, UK: Capstone.

Rozema, R. 2007. The Book Report, Version 2.0: Podcasting on Young Adult Novels. *The English Journal, 97*(1), 31–36. doi:10.2307/30047205.

Sewell, W. C., and Denton, S. 2011. Multimodal Literacies in the Secondary English Classroom. *English Journal, 100*(5), 61–65.

Smith, M., J. D. Wilhelm, and J. E. Fredricksen. 2012. *Oh, Yeah?! Putting Argument to Work Both in School and Out*. Portsmouth, NH: Heinemann.

Smythe, S., and P. Neufeld. 2010. "Podcast Time": Negotiating Digital Literacies and Communities of Learning in a Middle Years ELL Classroom. *Journal of Adolescent & Adult Literacy, 53*(6), 488–496.

Solomon, J. 2007, May 25. Pulling Back the Curtain. *On The Media*. NPR. Retrieved from www.onthemedia.org/2007/may/25/pulling-back-the-curtain.

Spence, L. K. 2009. Developing Multiple Literacies in a Website Project. *The Reading Teacher, 62*(7), 592–597. doi:10.1598/RT.62.7.5.

Spike Lee Quotes—BrainyQuote. n.d.. Retrieved August 18, 2012, from http://www.brainyquote.com/quotes/authors/s/spike_lee.html.

Spurlock, M. 2004. *Super Size Me*. Sony Pictures.

Sydell, L. 2011, November 10. Teen Study: Social Media Is Positive Experience. *NPR.org*. Retrieved from www.npr.org/2011/11/09/142166055/teen-study-social-media-is-positive-experience.

Tapscott, D. 2008. *Grown Up Digital: How the Net Generation Is Changing Your World HC* (1st ed.). New York: McGraw-Hill.

Tapscott, D., and A. D. Williams. 2006. *Wikinomics: How Mass Collaboration Changes Everything*. Portfolio Hardcover. Retrieved from www.amazon.com/dp/1591841380.

Tharp, T. L. 2010. Wiki, Wiki, Wiki—WHAT? Assessing Online Collaborative Writing. *English Journal, 99*(5), 40–46.

Theodosakis, N. 2001. *The Director in the Classroom: How Filmmaking Inspires Learning* (Book and CD). San Diego, CA: Tech4Learning, Inc.

Thomas, E. E., and K. Sassi. 2011. An Ethical Dilemma: Talking about Plagiarism and Academic Integrity in the Digital Age. *English Journal, 100*(6), 47–53.

Toastmasters International. 2011. *Your Speaking Voice: Tips for Adding Strength and Authority to Your Voice*. Retrieved from www.toastmasters.org/199-YourSpeakingVoice.

Tufte, E. R. 2006. *The Cognitive Style of PowerPoint: Pitching Out Corrupts Within, Second Edition* (2nd ed.). Cheshire, CT: Graphics Press.

Turkle, S. 2011. *Alone Together: Why We Expect More from Technology and Less from Each Other* (1st ed.). New York: Basic Books.

Turner, K. H. 2012. Digitalk as Community. *English Journal, 101*(4), 37–42.

University of Maryland Libraries. 2011, January. Evaluating Web Sites, UM Libraries. Retrieved August 13, 2012, from www.lib.umd.edu/guides/evaluate.html.

Warschauer, Mark. 2011. *Learning in the Cloud: How and Why to Transform Schools with Digital Media.* New York: Teachers College Press.

Whitney, A. E. 2011. In Search of the Authentic English Classroom: Facing the Schoolishness of School. *English Education, 44*(1), 51–62.

Wilber, D. J. 2010. *iWrite: Using Blogs, Wikis, and Digital Stories in the English Classroom* (1st ed.). Porstmouth, NH: Heinemann.

Wilhelm, J. D. 2010. Technology in Our Schools: A Call for a Cost/Benefit Analysis. *Voices from the Middle, 17*(3), 44–46.

Wilhelm, J. D., P. D. Friedemann, and J. Erickson. 1998. *Hyperlearning.* Portland, ME: Stenhouse Publishers.

Wilhelm, J. D., M. Smith, and J. E. Fredricksen. 2012. *Get It Done! Writing and Analyzing Informational Texts to Make Things Happen.* Portsmouth, NH: Heinemann.

Williams, M. 2012, August 17. In the Classroom: Live Oak Elementary School Students Produce Audio Podcasts | Edspace. *Edspace.* Retrieved September 6, 2012, from http://education.kqed.org/edspace/2012/08/17/in-the-classroom-live-oak-elementary-school-students-produce-audio-podcasts/.

Williams, R. 2008. *The Non-Designer's Design Book* (3rd ed.). Berkeley, CA: Peachpit Press.

Zemelman, S., H. Daniels, and A. Hyde. 2012. *Best Practice: Bringing Standards to Life in America's Classrooms* (4th ed.). Portsmouth, NH: Heinemann.

INDEX